SIMUL 2024

The Sixteenth International Conference on Advances in System Simulation

September 29 - October 03, 2024

Venice, Italy

SIMUL 2024 Editors

Carlo Simon, Hochschule Worms, Germany

Eric Innocenti, University of Corsica Pasquale Paoli, Corte, France

Printed from e-media with permission by:

Curran Associates, Inc.
57 Morehouse Lane
Red Hook, NY 12571

International Academy, Research, and Industry Association (IARIA)
412 Derby Way
Wilmington, DE 19810

Phone: (408) 893-6407
Fax: (408) 527-6351

petre@iaria.org

Additional copies of this publication are available from:

Curran Associates, Inc.
57 Morehouse Lane
Red Hook, NY 12571 USA
Phone: 845-758-0400
Fax: 845-758-2633
Email: curran@proceedings.com
Web: www.proceedings.com

Table of Contents

SIMUL 2024

Forward

The Siixteenth International Conference on Advances in System Simulation (SIMUL 2024), held on September 29 – October 3, 2024 in Venice, Italy, continued a series of events focusing on advances in simulation techniques and systems providing new simulation capabilities.

While different simulation events are already scheduled for years, SIMUL 2024 identified specific needs for ontology of models, mechanisms, and methodologies in order to make easy an appropriate tool selection. With the advent of Web Services and WEB 3.0 social simulation and human-in simulations bring new challenging situations along with more classical process simulations and distributed and parallel simulations. An update on the simulation tool considering these new simulation flavors was aimed at, too.

The conference provided a forum where researchers were able to present recent research results and new research problems and directions related to them. The conference sought contributions to stress-out large challenges in scale system simulation and advanced mechanisms and methodologies to deal with them. The accepted papers covered topics on social simulation, transport simulation, simulation tools and platforms, simulation methodologies and models, and distributed simulation.

We welcomed technical papers presenting research and practical results, position papers addressing the pros and cons of specific proposals, such as those being discussed in the standard forums or in industry consortiums, survey papers addressing the key problems and solutions on any of the above topics, short papers on work in progress, and panel proposals.

We take here the opportunity to warmly thank all the members of the SIMUL 2024 technical program committee as well as the numerous reviewers. The creation of such a broad and high quality conference program would not have been possible without their involvement. We also kindly thank all the authors that dedicated much of their time and efforts to contribute to the SIMUL 2024. We truly believe that thanks to all these efforts, the final conference program consists of top quality contributions.

This event could also not have been a reality without the support of many individuals, organizations and sponsors. We also gratefully thank the members of the SIMUL 2024 organizing committee for their help in handling the logistics and for their work that is making this professional meeting a success. We gratefully appreciate to the technical program committee co-chairs that contributed to identify the appropriate groups to submit contributions.

We hope the SIMUL 2024 was a successful international forum for the exchange of ideas and results between academia and industry and to promote further progress in simulation research. . We also hope that Venice provided a pleasant environment during the conference and everyone saved some time for exploring this beautiful city

SIMUL 2024 Steering Committee

Carlo Simon, Hochschule Worms - University of Applied Sciences, Germany
Frank Herrmann, University of Applied Sciences Regensburg, Germany
Sibylle Fröschle, TUHH - Hamburg University of Technology, Germany

SIMUL 2024 Publicity Chair

Lorena Parra Boronat, Universitat Politecnica de Valencia, Spain
Sandra Viciano Tudela, Universitat Politecnica de Valencia, Spain
Jose Miguel Jimenez, Universitat Politecnica de Valencia, Spain
Francisco Javier Díaz Blasco, Universitat Politecnica de Valencia, Spain
Ali Ahmad, Universitat Politecnica de Valencia, Spain

SIMUL 2024

Committee

SIMUL 2024 Steering Committee

Carlo Simon, Hochschule Worms - University of Applied Sciences, Germany
Frank Herrmann, University of Applied Sciences Regensburg, Germany
Sibylle Fröschle, TUHH - Hamburg University of Technology, Germany

SIMUL 2024 Publicity Chair

Lorena Parra Boronat, Universitat Politecnica de Valencia, Spain
Sandra Viciano Tudela, Universitat Politecnica de Valencia, Spain
Jose Miguel Jimenez, Universitat Politecnica de Valencia, Spain
Francisco Javier Díaz Blasco, Universitat Politecnica de Valencia, Spain
Ali Ahmad, Universitat Politecnica de Valencia, Spain

SIMUL 2024 Technical Program Committee

Petra Ahrweiler, Johannes Gutenberg University Mainz, Germany
Saleh Abdel-Afou Alaliyat, Norwegian University of Science and Technology, Norway
Chrissanthi Angeli, University of West Attica, Greece
Ozgur M. Araz, College of Business | University of Nebraska–Lincoln, USA
Alfonso Ariza Quintana, University of Malaga, Spain
Natesh B. Arunachalam, The University of Texas at Austin, USA
Michel Audette, Old Dominion University, USA
Souvik Barat, Tata Consultancy Services Research, India
Ana Paula Barbosa Póvoa, Universidade de Lisboa, Portugal
Marek Bauer, Politechnika Krakowska, Poland
Sahil Belsare, Walmart / Northeastern University, USA
Massimo Bertolini, University of Modena and Reggio Emilia - UNIMORE, Italy
John Betts, Monash University, Australia
Maria Julia Blas, Instituto de Desarrollo y Diseño (INGAR) | UTN-CONICET, Argentina
Paolo Bocciarelli, University of Rome Tor Vergata, Italy
Stefan Bosse, University of Bremen, Germany
Jalil Boudjadar, Aarhus University, Denmark
Christos Bouras, University of Patras, Greece
Lelio Campanile, Università degli Studi della Campania "L. Vanvitelli", Italy
Yuxin Chen, University of California, Davis, USA
Franco Cicirelli, ICAR-CNR, Italy
Fábio Coelho, CEG-IST Instituto Superior Técnico | University of Lisbon, Portugal
Federico Concone, University of Palermo, Italy
Duilio Curcio, University of Calabria, Italy
Andrea D'Ambrogio, University of Roma TorVergata, Italy

Gabriele D'Angelo, University of Bologna, Italy
Luis Antonio de Santa-Eulalia, Business School | Université de Sherbrooke, Canada
Daniel Delahaye, ENAC LAB, Toulouse, France
Alexander Ditter, Friedrich-Alexander University Erlangen-Nürnberg (FAU), Germany
Anatoli Djanatliev, University of Erlangen-Nuremberg, Germany
Julie Dugdale, University Grenoble Alps, France
Mahmoud Elbattah, Université de Picardie Jules Verne, France
Sabeur Elkosantini, University of Carthage, Tunisia
Amr Eltawil, School of Innovative Design Engineering / Japan University of Science and Technology, Egypt
Diego Encinas, Informatics Research Institute LIDI - CIC - UNLP, Argentina
Fouad Erchiqui, Université du Québec en Abitibi-Témiscamingue, Canada
Zuhal Erden, Atilim University, Turkey
Mourad Fakhfakh, University of Sfax, Tunisia
Javier Faulin, Public University of Navarra, Spain
Sibylle Fröschle, TU Hamburg, Germany
José Manuel Galán, Universidad de Burgos, Spain
Ramo Galeano, Universidad Autonoma de Barcelona, Spain
Erol Gelenbe, Institute of Theoretical and Applied Informatics of the Polish Academy of Sciences, Poland
Simon Genser, Virtual Vehicle Research GmbH, Graz, Austria
Katja Gilly de la Sierra-Llamazares, Universidad Miguel Hernández, Spain
Apostolos Gkamas, University of Ioannina, Greece
Denis Gracanin, Virginia Tech, USA
Antoni Grau, Technical University of Catalonia, Barcelona, Spain
Andrew Greasley, Aston University, Birmingham, UK
Feng Gu, The College of Staten Island, CUNY, USA
Nikolos Gurney, University of Southern California | Institute for Creative Technologies, USA
Stefan Haag, University of Applied Sciences Worms, Germany
Petr Hanáček, Brno University of Technology, Czech Republic
Magdalena Hańderek, Cracow University of Technology, Poland
Thomas Hanne, University of Applied Sciences and Arts Northwestern Switzerland / Institute for Information Systems, Switzerland
Eduardo Hargreaves, Petrobras, Brazil
Frank Herrmann, University of Applied Sciences Regensburg, Germany
Tsan-sheng Hsu, Institute of Information Science | Academia Sinica, Taiwan
Xiaolin Hu, Georgia State University, Atlanta, USA
Marc-Philippe Huget, Polytech Annecy-Chambery-LISTIC | University of Savoie, France
Shahid Hussain, Penn State Behrend, USA
Mauro Iacono, Università degli Studi della Campania "Luigi Vanvitelli", Italy
Lisa Jackson, Loughborough University, UK
Maria João Viamonte, Institute of Engineering (ISEP) - Polytechnic Institute of Porto (IPP), Portugal
Peter Kemper, William & Mary, USA
Yun Bae Kim, Sungkyunkwan University (SKKU), Korea
Youngjae Kim, Sogang University, Seoul, Korea
Hildegarde Koen, Council for Scientific and Industrial Research (CSIR), South Africa
Dmitry G. Korzun, Petrozavodsk State University | Institute of Mathematics and Information Technology, Russia
Mouna Kotti, University of Gabes, Tunisia

Vladik Kreinovich, University of Texas at El Paso, USA
Anatoly Kurkovsky, Georgia Gwinnett College - Greater Atlanta University System of Georgia, USA
Massimo La Scala, Politecnico di Bari, Italy
Ettore Lanzarone, University of Bergamo, Italy
Herman Le Roux, Council for Scientific and Industrial Research (CSIR), South Africa
Fedor Lehocki, Slovak University of Technology in Bratislava, Slovakia
Stephan Leitner, University of Klagenfurt, Austria
Laurent Lemarchand, University of Brest (UBO), France
António M. Lopes, University of Porto, Portugal
Fabian Lorig, Malmö University | IoTaP, Sweden
Emilio Luque, University Autonoma of Barcelona (UAB), Spain
Johannes Lüthi, University of Applied Sciences - Fachhochschule Kufstein Tirol, Austria
Imran Mahmood, Brunel University London, UK
Fahad Maqbool, University of Sargodha, Pakistan
Eda Marchetti, ISTI-CNR, Pisa, Italy
Romolo Marotta, University of Rome "Sapienza", Italy
Omar Masmali, The University of Texas, El Paso, USA
Michele Mastroianni, Università degli Studi della Campania "Luigi Vanvitelli", Italy
Andrea Matta, Politecnico di Milano, Italy
Radek Matušů, Tomas Bata University in Zlin, Czech Republic
Roger McHaney, Kansas State University, USA
Nuno Melão, Polytechnic Institute of Viseu, Portugal
Roderick Melnik, MS2Discovery Interdisciplinary Research Institute | Wilfrid *Laurier* University, Canada
Adel Mhamdi, RWTH Aachen University, Germany
Owen Molloy, National University of Ireland, Galway, Ireland
Mahathir Monjur, University of North Carolina at Chapel Hill, USA
Sébastien Monnet, LISTIC / Savoie Mont Blanc University, France
Federico Montori, University of Bologna, Italy
Jérôme Morio, ONERA (the French Aerospace Lab), France
Paulo Moura Oliveira, Universidade de Trás-os-Montes e Alto Douro (UTAD) / INESC-TEC Porto, Portugal
Andrzej Mycek, Cracow University of Technology, Poland
Nazmun Nahar, University of Jyvaskyla, Finland
Luis Gustavo Nardin, National College of Ireland, Ireland
James J. Nutaro, Oak Ridge National Laboratory, USA
Alessandro Pellegrini, Sapienza University of Rome, Italy
Tomas Potuzak, University of West Bohemia, Czech Republic
Manon Prédhumeau, Grenoble Alps University, France
Dipak Pudasaini, Tribhuvan University, Nepal / Ryerson University, Canada
Francesco Quaglia, University of Rome Tor Vergata, Italy
Abdul Rahman, Deloitte, USA
Marco Remondino, Università degli Studi di Genova, Italy
Dupas Rémy, University of Bordeaux, France
Oscar Rodríguez Polo, University of Alcala, Spain
Kristin Yvonne Rozier, Iowa State University, USA
Cristina Ruiz Martin, Carleton University, Canada
Julio Sahuquillo, Universitat Politecnica de Valencia, Spain
Nandakishore Santhi, Los Alamos National Laboratory, USA
Victorino Sanz, ETSI Informática | UNED, Spain

Paulo Jorge Sequeira Goncalves, Instituto Politecnico de Castelo Branco, Portugal
Li Shi, Snap Inc., USA
Patrick Siarry, Université Paris-Est Créteil (UPEC), France
Carlo Simon, Hochschule Worms - University of Applied Sciences, Germany
Leszek Siwik, AGH-UST University of Science and Technology, Krakow, Poland
Yuri N. Skiba, Universidad Nacional Autónoma de México, Mexico
Azeddien M. Sllame, University of Tripoli, Libya
Giandomenico Spezzano, CNR-ICAR, Italy
Sven Spieckermann, SimPlan AG, Germany
Renata Spolon Lobato, UNESP - São Paulo State University, Brazil
Mu-Chun Su, National Central University, Taiwan
Grażyna Suchacka, University of Opole, Poland
János Száz, Corvinus University, Hungary
Kumar Tamma, University of Minnesota, USA
Ingo J. Timm, Trier University, Germany
Felix Tischer, Virtual Vehicle Research GmbH, Austria
Abtin Tondar, Stanford University School of Medicine, USA
Klaus G. Troitzsch, University of Koblenz-Landau, retired, Germany
Hasan Turan, University of New South Wales, Australia
Alfonso Urquía, UNED, Spain
Edson L. Ursini, University of Campinas - Technology School, Brazil
Vahab Vahdatzad, Harvard Medical School, Boston, USA
Bert Van Acker, University of Antwerp, Belgium
Durk-Jouke van der Zee, University of Groningen, Netherlands
Antonio Virdis, University of Pisa, Italy
Frank Werner, OvGU Magdeburg, Germany
Kuan Yew Wong, Universiti Teknologi Malaysia (UTM), Malaysia
Yang Yang, Cornell University, USA
Irina Yatskiv (Jackiva), Transport and Telecommunication Institute, Latvia
Lara Zakfeld, Hochschule Worms, Germany

Copyright Information

Weld Data Collecting for Use in Welding Simulations and Digital Twins

Martin Gredehall
Department of Mathematics and Natural Sciences
Blekinge Institute of Technology
Karlskrona, Sweden
e-mail: martin.gredehall@bth.se

Prof. Dr. Tobias Larsson
Department of Mechanical Engineering
Blekinge Institute of Technology
Karlskrona, Sweden
e-mail: tobias.larsson@bth.se

Abstract— **Today´s industry produces a lot of pipes; for cooling, chemicals and other purposes. The piping can be in a large variety of dimensions and materials, with stainless steel being a common choice due to its resistance to corrosion. Ships, submarines or powerplants, can have several kilometres of piping, with high demands and requirements on quality and safety. Over the lifetime of a pipe, maintenance or replacement may be necessary, often requiring welding to join sections. Due to economic considerations, much of the fabrication is conducted in workshops, necessitating precise tolerances and robust processes, but also causing problems when on-site installation is needed. This study aims to collect measurement data for subsequent use in welding simulations and the development of digital twins for expected final design. Tree pipes were welded with orbital TIG-welding and during the welding, temperature was measured with type-k thermocouples around the diameter of the pipe. Before and after the welding the length of the pipes was measured in four places. Test data collected includes temperature profiles and shrinkage during welding. The tests revealed longitudinal shrinkage in the weld zone ranging from 0.12% to 0.18% of the length of the pipe, with higher heat input resulting in increased longitudinal shrinkage. In the future, this measurement data can be used for verification purposes in the development of digital twin models by comparing actual welding outcomes with simulation results, aiding the prediction and resolution of geometric tolerance challenges during production, and installation. This paper proposes an approach to collect data for future simulation and prediction of deformation and shrinkage in piping systems during welding using digital twins.**

Keywords- welding; orbital welding; simulation; TIG; design.

I. INTRODUCTION

Much of today's industry is depending on pipes both for production and for their products. Hence, piping could be a significant part of the production time for a plant or product. As an example, time consumption for pipe machining and installation in ship construction accounts for 9-18% of total hours of which half of the working hours are used for assembling and welding various flanges and pipes [1]. In brewery processing plants, much brewing equipment is factory-built. However, many of the small-bore pipes and their interconnections are brought from manufacturers and joined on-site [2].

For joining pipes into systems of pipes, welding is one of the most used joining techniques. Welding is a critical joining process in the manufacturing process. Circumferential welding joints are commonly used in marine engineering, nuclear power plant and aerospace industry. For hight-strength welding of these structures, Tungsten Inert Gas welding (TIG) is a popular joining technique [3].

For pipework, the preferred method is automatic orbital welding. If properly programmed, an orbital welding machine is capable of consistently produce high-quality welds [4]. For the welding in biopharmaceutical, brewery, and related industries the welding without filler material is the most common, even though welding with filler material exists. Since TIG-welding is using a non-consumable tungsten electrode to produce the heat for the weld the filler material is added separately to the heat input [2]. When using welding as a joining method there will be a Heat Affected Zone (HAZ). The HAZ that results from the welding operations should be minimized [2].This is because the heat from the welding can change the structure of the material and affect the material properties.

Joining with welding can sometime be difficult. Some factors leading to poor welds is pipe geometry as pipes are manufactured to outer diameter (OD). Wall thickness and ovality tolerances that affect the alignment of pipe ends [8]. With better and stronger materials, the focus has moved to greater fabrication challenges like structures fabricated from thinner and lighter sections, which were previously masked by mass [2].

On-site welds are often inaccessible from the inside, so site welding is more difficult to control. Inadequately welded joints can compromise product quality [2]. Also, the fabricators centroid misalignment may be an important factor for the product quality. Good orbital welding requires matched pipes, which are correctly aligned and a minimum overlap of 95%, preferably in the range 90-100 ± 10% [2]. Figure 1 below shows the orbital TIG welding head mounted on a pipe. The picture is taken during the welding.

Figure 1. Orbital TIG Welding head mounted on a pipe during experiments.

Pipes are manufactured in two distinct ways – as welded pipes or seamless pipes. Commercially pipes are sold with manufacturing tolerances in ovality and wall thickness. This results in pipes and tubes that are neither circular nor of even wall thickness [2].

As the requirements continue to increase, the challenge of keeping a fabrication process within tolerance becomes more difficult. At some point it is no longer feasible to approach each individual assembly of parts with identical settings and process parameters. Small differences at the part level makes every assembly unique and to reliably achieve a good outcome, each assembly will require small adjustments. This is commonly referred to ass mass customization, meaning that each product is approached individually rather than interchangeably [5]. In all production, tolerances could be a challenge during assembling. In a piping system with several joints and bends, there will be many possibilities for quality and geometrical problems. Most companies are fully aware of the fact that a change is costlier in production than in the design phase [6]. To minimise the cost for geometrical variation, geometry assurance can be helpful.

Geometry assurance can be described as a set of activities that contributes to minimizing the effect of geometrical variation in the final product. Activities take place in all phases of the product realization loop. The phases where geometrical assurance is to take place is design phase, pre-production phase, production phase [7]. To foresee, and thereby also possibly reduce, this kind of problems in a final assembly, methods to predict geometrical variation are crucial tools [8]. To verify the geometry inspection, inspection points are used. In early production series and prototypes those are often more in numbers to gain knowledge and understanding of the product. Later production has often fewer inspection points to reduce resources thanks to quicker inspection procedure and simplified analysis of measurement data. By reducing the number of inspection point there are a risk of losing to much information about the manufacturing process. This risk can be much lesser by using a structured method for the inspection point reduction [9].

Figure 2 below shows an example of a piping system for a submarine.

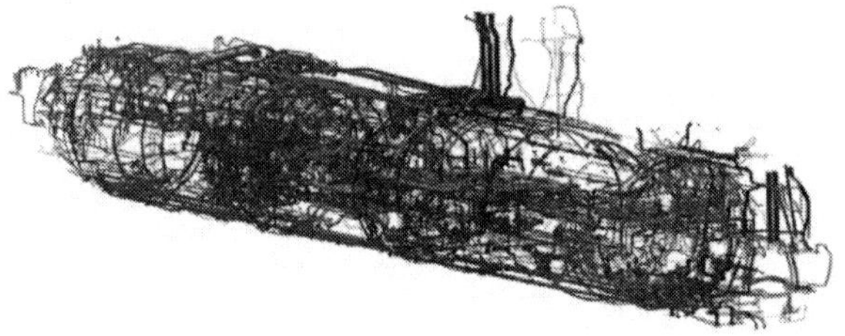

Figure 2. Piping system for a submarine. There are about 10.000 pipe components in a submarine like the Swedish A26 that must be able to handle high pressure, liquid, and toxic gases. Picture Copyright SAAB AB[10]

With a digital twin, mirroring a piping system, with all the weld joints, it should be possible to predict the weld temperatures, shrinkage, and deformation from the weld zones in the whole system by simulating the welding. Differences in shrinkage and deformation due to changes in heat input during welding should be possible to simulate for the whole piping system. With potential shrinkage in the weld zone there is a possibility of large amount of shrinking and deformation for the whole piping system. If the welding order will affect the shrinkage and deformation in a welded piping system, this can be studied during simulation.

Hence, the research questions that guide the work in this paper are;

- RQ1: Will it be possible to collect temperature data from welding that later can be used for welding simulation in a digital twin?
- RQ2: Will it be possible to measure longitudinal shrinkage on a thin wall stainless pipe after orbital welding so that the data can be used in welding simulation?

The paper is organized as follows. The method is described in Section 2. In Section 3 the results are shown. Section 4 contains discussion and in Section 5 conclusions and future work are presented.

II. METHOD

The research is case based [11] and using applied cases/experiments to justify the conclusions. The process approach for simulation and testing is shown in Figure 3 below. Before and after welding there will be measuring to see how the part changes. Optimisation will be done when needed and this will be mirrored in a digital twin in later work. For this paper, the part marked in the red zone in the sketch of the process, are made.

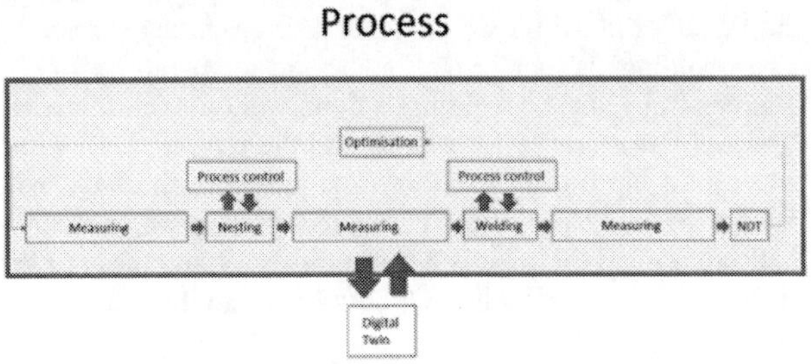

Figure 3. Process.

The pipes are measured before and after welding to see the longitudinal shrinkage in the pipe from the welding. Also, the temperatures are measured in chosen places during the welding. From this information the process will be optimised for each weld with new welding parameters. After each welding the weld will be checked visually (NDT - Non destructive testing). Then the information can be used in a digital twin.

A. *Material*

The base material used in this experiment are stainless steel 316L (1.4404). The welded material is a pipe with the outer diameter 88.9 mm and a wall thickness of 2 mm. The pipe is seamless for less interfering with the weld.

B. *Welding equipment*

The welding is done with automatic orbital TIG-welding. The welding Machine is an AMI model 415A from Arc Machines Inc. The backing gas used was Formier 10 with the flow rate of 10 l/min. The welding head for the weld test is an Arc Machine Inc. model 15 shown in Figure 4 below.

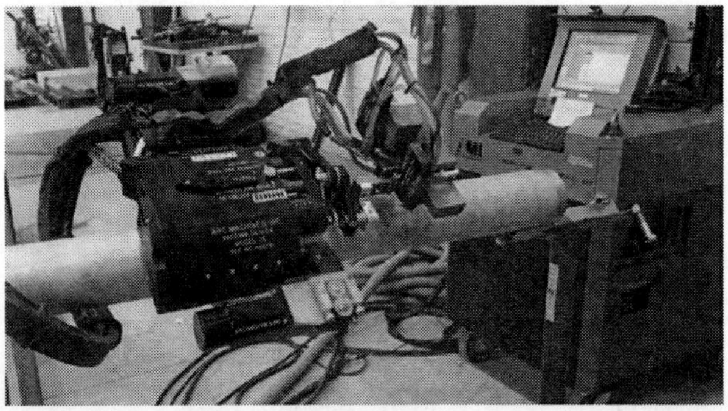

Figure 4. Welding head, Arc Machines Inc. Mod. 15.

Figures 5 and 6 below show the placement of the thermocouples during welding. Figure 5 shows test 1 and Figure 6 test 2 and 3. Welding direction is clockwise. The first thermocouple is placed 10 mm from the weld centre. Then the following thermocouples are placed 15 mm, 20 mm and 25 mm from the weld centre. 25 mm is only in test 2 and 3.

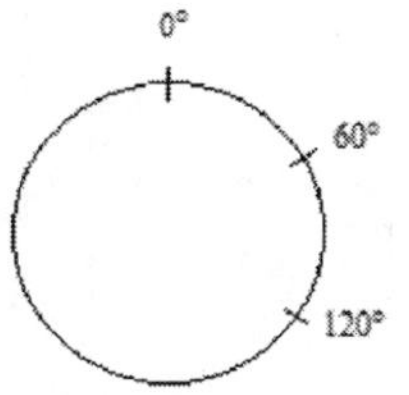

Figure 5. Placement of thermocouples. Test one.

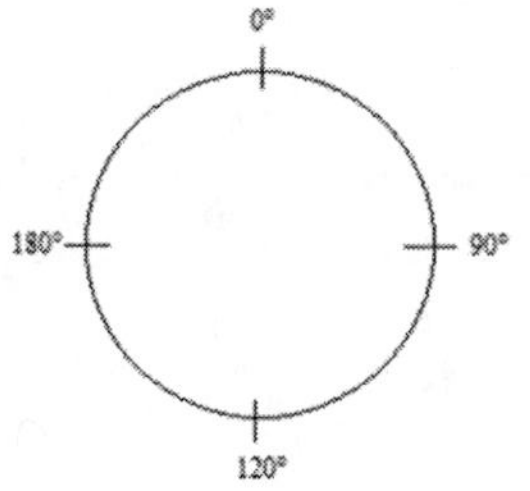

Figure 6. placement of thermocouples. Test 2 and 3.

C. *Measuring*

The measuring of the length of the pipes are done before nesting, after nesting and after welding. The procedure is shown in Figure 7 below.

Figure 7. Measuring of pipe.

D. Welding parameters

Tables I and II below shows the welding parameters used during the welding.

TABLE I WELDING PARAMETERS

	Volts (V)	High Amp	High Pulse	Low Amp	Low Pulse
Test 1	8.3	100	0.15	47	0.13
Test 2	8.3	100	0.15	47	0.13
Test 3	8.3	108	0.15	55	0.13

TABLE II WELDING PARAMETERS

	Downslope	mm/min	Energy (kJ/mm)
Test 1	0	80	0.40
Test 2	0	80	0.47
Test 3	0	80	0.52

E. Thermal conductors

For this experiment thermocouples of type K was used. Type K thermocouples consists of two wires of dissimilar metals joined together at one end, called the measurement ("hot") junction. The other end is connected to the signal conditioning circuitry traces, typically made of copper. The junction between the thermocouples metals and the copper traces is called the reference ("cold") junction. The Voltage produced at the reference junction depends on the temperatures at both the measurement junction and the reference junction [12] (see Figure 8).

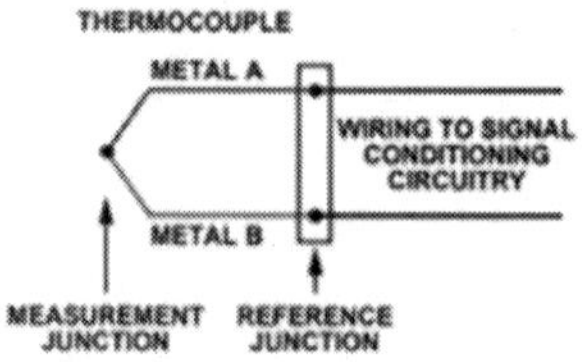

Figure 8. Thermocouple.

F. Welding case

Two 300 mm seamless tubes of stainless steel 316 with a wall thickness of 2 mm are welded together using an automatic orbital TIG-welding machine described above. The welding is performed at room temperature of 23 degrees Celsius. The welding is done without welding wire. The welding starts at 12 o´clock and the pipe is turning one and a half lap during welding. The arc from the weld will always be at 12 o´clock. The choice of welding one and a half lap around the pipe is because of the straightness of the finished pipe. Figure 9 below shows welding direction.

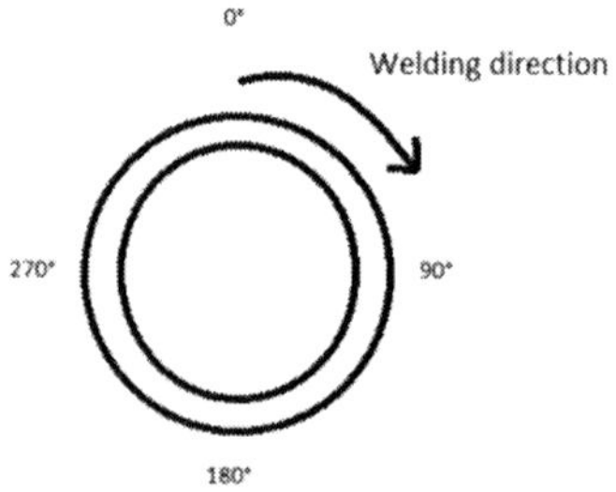

Figure 9. Welding direction.

III. RESULTS

The results from the welding show that there is 0.12% to 0.18% of shrinkage in the weld zone when measured before and after welding. It also shows that with increased heat input the shrinkage will increase. Tables 3-5 show the measuring results from the longitudinal shrinkage in mm with results of 0.7-1.1 mm in shrinkage. Tables 6-8 shows temperature results from welding in degrees Celsius, with maximum temperatures measured from 520 degrees Celsius to 640 degrees Celsius for the different weld tests.

The straightness of the pipes after welding is shown in Figure 11 and all the pipes were after welding straight.

TABLE III MEASURMENTS SHRINKAGE

Test one						
(mm)	0°	90°	180°	270°	Mean value	Mean shrink.
Measurement before welding	589,5	598,1	598,1	598,4	598,3	0,12%
Measurement after welding	597,6	597,6	597,5	597,5	597,6	0,7 mm

TABLE IV MEASURMENTS SHRINKAGE

Test two						
(mm)	0°	90°	180°	270°	Mean value	Mean shrink.
Measurement before welding	604,5	604,6	604,2	604,6	604,5	0,15%
Measurement after welding	603,8	603,3	603,3	604	603,6	0,9 mm

TABLE V MEASURMENTS SHRINKAGE

Test tree						
(mm)	0°	90°	180°	270°	Mean value	Mean shrink.
Measurement before welding	598,1	598	598,2	598,5	598,2	0,18%
Measurement after welding	597	596,6	597,1	597,6	597,1	1,1 mm

TABLE VI MEASUREMENT TEMPERATURE

Test 1			
Weld start 315°, this weld was visually OK			
Placement of thermocouple	0°	60°	120°
mm from centre of weld	10	15	20
Temperature in Celsius lap 1	582	427	322
Temperature in Celsius lap 2	604	491	394

TABLE VII MEASUREMENT TEMPERATURE

Test 2				
Weld start 0°, this weld was visually OK				
Placement of thermocouple	0°	90°	180°	270°
mm from centre of weld	10	15	20	25
Temperature in Celsius lap 1	443	351	276	176
Temperature in Celsius lap 2	520	442	265	-

TABLE VIII MEASUREMENT TEMPERATURE

Test 3				
Weld start 0°, This weld was visually not OK				
Placement of thermocouple	0°	90°	180°	270°
mm from centre of weld	10	15	20	25
Temperature in Celsius lap 1	493	487	330	284
Temperature in Celsius lap 2	639	392	304	-

Figure 11 shows the straightness of the pipe after welding.

Figure 11. Straightness in pipe after welding.

IV. DISCUSSION

The results show a longitudinal shrinkage of 0.12%-0,18% witch if several welds are added can end up in a total longitudinal shrinkage of several millimetres and even centimetres. For large systems of pipes this will be a significant aspect during design and construction. To be able to simulate this in the beginning of the design, will be worth a lot of time in the end of production, as predictions of outcome and hence also compensation may be made early, something that is enabled via the research in this paper.

The literature review indicates that there is a need for geometry assurance in larger sections of piping systems on ships, submarines, powerplants and other facilities. One way of doing this is to simulate the welding. To be able to do this comparation data is needed. In this paper we looked specifically at welding joints, with orbital TIG welding experiments, with the aim of collecting data for later simulation of weld joints via digital twins and adding the possibility to adapt design parameters already before the production is performed. The shrinkage in the weld test behaved as expected, even though there is a small possibility that there are problems with the measuring equipment that will give small differences.

The temperature was measured with thermocouple type K, those were calibrated at zero degrees Celsius and at one hundred degrees Celsius with good results, within two degrees Celsius. Still there is a small possibility for errors if there for example is an air pocket between the thermocouple and the base material during welding. The pipe was, as shown in Figure 11, straight after the welding.

V. CONCLUSIONS AND FUTURE WORK

Data from weld test shows that there is longitudinal shrinking in the weld area during welding of pipes in 316L, with a diameter of 89.9 mm and wall thickness of 2 mm. The shrinkage from the tests is 0.12-0.18% of the length and with a large amount of weld joints, this can be significant for the possibility of mounting the part. In a piping system this can add up to several millimetres or even centimetres.

Future work is development of simulation models that will mirror the actual welding for digital twinning purposes. Through those simulations prediction of deformations and shrinkage during welding can be performed. When constructing the simulations verification will be made by comparing the simulations with the experiments in this paper. When the simulation models are made, they will be inserted in models of sections from piping systems. This way it will be possible to simulate how several welds in a piping system will affect the end product and plan the production from the data given in the simulation. Different geometries, materials and numbers of welds can then be simulated in advance to help plan production. By doing those simulations before welding, the time and quality in production will increase and it will be easier to prefabricate piping systems with less time for on-site welding.

Acknowledgement

I would like to thank the company Tech Weld Sweden AB in Karlshamn, Sweden, for their help with the welding and all the other things they helped with around the practical experiment.

REFERENCES

[1] Q. Wu, Y. Mao, J. Chen, and C. Wang, 'Application research of digital twin-driven ship intelligent manufacturing system: Pipe machining production line', *J. Mar. Sci. Eng.*, vol. 9, no. 3, 2021, doi: 10.3390/jmse9030338.

[2] T. A. Mamvura, A. E. Paterson, and D. Fanucchi, 'The impact of pipe geometry variations on hygiene and success of orbital welding of brewing industry equipment', *J Inst Brew*, pp. 81–97, 2017, doi: 10.1002/jib.398.

[3] H. Arora, K. M. Basha, D. N. Abhishek, and B. Devesh, 'Welding simulation of circumferential weld joint using TIG welding process', presented at the Materials Today: Proceedings, 2021, pp. 923–929. doi: 10.1016/j.matpr.2021.06.315.

[4] G. J. Curiel, G. Hauser, P. Peschel, and D. A. Timperlay, 'Hygenic equipment design criteria', *Trends Food Sci Tech*, vol. 1993, no. 4, pp. 225–229.

[5] H. Hultman, S. Cedergren, K. Wärmefjord, and R. Söderberg, 'Predicting Geometrical Variation in Fabricated Assemblies Using a Digital Twin Approach Including a Novel Non-Nominal Welding Simulation', *Aerospace*, vol. 9, no. 9, 2022, doi: 10.3390/aerospace9090512.

[6] R. Söderberg, L. Lindkvist, K. Wärmefjord, and J. S. Carlson, 'Virtual Geometry Assurance Process and Toolbox', presented at the Procedia CIRP, 2016, pp. 3–12. doi: 10.1016/j.procir.2016.02.043.

[7] R. Söderberg, K. Wärmefjord, J. S. Carlson, and L. Lindkvist, 'Toward a Digital Twin for real-time geometry assurance in individualized production', *CIRP Ann. - Manuf. Technol.*, vol. 66, no. 1, pp. 137–140, 2017, doi: 10.1016/j.cirp.2017.04.038.

[8] R. Söderberg, K. Wärmefjord, L. Lindkvist, and R. Berlin, 'The influence of spot weld position variation on geometrical quality', *CIRP Ann. - Manuf. Technol.*, vol. 61, no. 1, pp. 13–16, 2012, doi: 10.1016/j.cirp.2012.03.127.

[9] K. Wärmefjord, J. S. Carlson, and R. Söderberg, 'An investigation of the effect of sample size on geometrical inspection point reduction using cluster analysis', *CIRP J. Manuf. Sci. Technol.*, vol. 3, no. 3, pp. 227–235, 2010, doi: 10.1016/j.cirpj.2010.12.001.

[10] 'Piping system for a submarine'. SAAB AB, 20240522. [Online]. Available: https://www.saab.com/newsroom/stories/2020/july/a-submarine-in-space

[11] R. K. Yin, *Case study research: design and methods*, 5. London: SAGE, 2014. [Online]. Available: https://go.exlibris.link/lvTrXkpY

[12] M. Duff and J. Towey, 'Two Ways to Measure Temperature Using Thermocouples Feature Simplicity, Accuracy, and Flexibility', *Analog Dialogue*, vol. 2010 vol 44, oct.

A Computer Vision Based Tracking Framework for Medical Training

Bo Sun
Department of Computer Science
Rowan University
Glassboro, NJ, USA
e-mail: sunb@rowan.edu

Lucas Grebe
Department of Computer Science
Rowan University
Glassboro, NJ, USA
e-mail: grebel42@students.rowan.edu

***Abstract*— Medical simulation often utilizes standardized patients or mannequins to train and assess medical students. We present a computer vision-based framework where we can accurately augment virtual pathology to a standardized patient/mannequin. The framework offers a unique marker-based tracking approach using the computer vision method, which delivers a fast and precise augmentation for a simulated cranial (head) ultrasound prototype. The technique is very efficient and cost-effective compared with other tracking approaches.**

Keywords-medical simulation; computer vision; human computer interaction framework.

I. INTRODUCTION

According to the Safe Healthcare blog of the US Centers for Disease Control and Prevention (CDC) [1], more people die from medical errors and related issues than from lack of access to medical services. In the US, unintentional injury, including medical errors, kills more than 400,000 people annually [1]. Medical simulation, a computer-based simulation technique, has been widely adopted by medical schools to strengthen clinical skills by increasing indirect patient-related practices. The simulation techniques often use mannequins and Standardized Patients (SPs) to produce a realistic training scenario. However, since most SPs/mannequins are "healthy" individuals, medical pathologies are added via computer simulation. Depending on the diagnosis procedures, rendering of the simulated pathology based on the movement of a diagnostic tool (such as a stethoscope or an ultrasound scanner) requires a fast and precise tracking approach.

Many traditional simulations use electromagnetic trackers, which include a heavy magnetic device, reference cube, and marker, to enable tracking. This tracking system has space and environment requirements and is often connected with long cables. Other simulations involve haptic devices, where the force and movement of medical devices are tracked. These devices are typically heavy-duty and very expensive, depending on the tracking accuracy required by the simulator.

To make the simulation more portable, we present a Computer Vision-based Tracking (CVT) technique in this paper. The system can be carried around easily and offers a cost-effective solution compared to a magnetic tracker and haptic device. The new approach permits a more convenient way for medical training and assessment.

The CVT system consists of a camera and a box-shape marker. The technique uses OpenCV to detect the marker and produce translation and rotation vectors related to the marker. We applied a subtraction factor to increase the tracking space limitation of one camera. Comparing with existing optical based tracking techniques that often use multiple cameras or other sensor devices, our CVT only adopted one camera and relies on a unique box shape marker to ensure the tracking accuracy. The new approach permits a medical trainee to conduct training at any chosen location, such as home, office and lab, using a laptop with a build-in camera. In contrast, traditional optical setting involving multicamera or sensors often requires dedicated lab space to support the training since the set up requires specific distances and angles among the devices.

The framework was applied to a cranial (head) ultrasound prototype using a 3D brain mesh model. The system runs efficiently and accurately to produce an ultrasound slice when examining a brain.

The paper will present the related work in Section 2, detail the method in Section 3, summarize the results in Section 4, and conclude the study in Section 5.

II. RELATED WORKS

Medical simulation techniques could produce two types of outcomes depending on the stage of development. One is a research prototype, likely produced by higher education. This type of work can be retrieved through paper publication. The other is a commercial simulator. Its technique is not available for the reproduction of research; therefore, has little value to the research community.

The tracking techniques generally used by medical simulation are 1) electromagnetic tracker, 2) haptic device, and 3) optical tracking [2]. Therefore, we separate our reviews into these areas in this section. We will focus on tracking techniques often seen in ultrasound simulation initially, then detail optical tracking usage in general medical simulation.

A. Tracking Techniques in Ultrasound Simulation

Schallware Ultrasound Simulator [3] adopted a mannequin and several dummy probes connected with a magnetic tracker. The simulator system consists of pre-collected clinic pathological data as training cases in internal medicine, cardiology, obstetrics, and gynecology. Simbionix ultrasound mentor [4] is a high-fidelity simulator. The system uses magnetic tracking techniques along with mock probes to scan mannequins in developing ultrasound training for different genders and ages for various medical specialties.

As seen in these commercial simulators' manuals and brochures, magnetic tracking equipment is used to support the tracking. The probes from both simulators connect with a heavy-duty cable to track the device's movement precisely. In addition, the sensitivity of the magnetic tracking can be quickly impacted by other metal particles nearby, as described in [5].

Other commercial simulators use haptic devices as input interfaces. The device uses electric sensors to monitor the hand motion of trainees along with the force applied to the device. So, haptic devices are commonly seen among simulators. ScanTrainer [6], a transvaginal and transabdominal ultrasound simulation, adopted a haptic device to deliver the training. They used a virtual patient to mimic a physical body. To study the skills, a trainee must watch two monitors (one for simulated ultrasound and one for VR patient). The tracking is completely handled by the haptic device without visual indicators.

The most recent development from Surgical Science uses VR techniques [7] that adopted optical tracking embedded in the VR headset to monitor the movement of mock devices, which permits trainees to complete the entire training in VR.

Neither haptic devices nor VR headsets are feasible devices for developing a low-cost portable system. Therefore, the field needs an optical tracking platform to support the future development of ultrasound simulation.

B. Optical Tracking

Markov-Vetter et al. created an ultrasound simulation, CranUS [8], based on optical tracking. The system simulates cranial (head) ultrasound for infants. However, the simulation focused on the training outcomes and had no details about the optical tracking techniques used in the research prototype. According to a figure illustration of the paper, they adopted two large overhead-mounted cameras to visually track the operational space of the scanning. Duan et al. [9] created a 3D tracking system using three cameras and two markers for a virtual surgery simulation. The system obtained 3D coordinates of each marker for every two cameras, then used the average of six coordinates produced by three pairs of camera groups to archive accurate 3D coordination. OptiTrack [10], a commercial optical tracking system, requires multiple high-end overhead cameras. The system has less accuracy compared with a laser tracking system, SteamVR, according to [11]. After all, none of these techniques are portable when multiple cameras are involved. Volutracer O.P.U.S. [12] is a relatively new commercial ultrasound simulator that uses optical tracking. It adopts a web camera, a mock transducer, a marker, and a cardboard to mimic ultrasound scanning. The system is portable and convenient for trainees. However, its tracking technique is not publicly available since it is a commercial simulator. Nevertheless, Optical Tracking Systems (OTS) are often used as surgical tools to register computer-added images for surgical navigation, as seen in Lee et al.'s work [13]. These commercial OTS [10] [14] [15] often use other techniques, such as near-infrared light or senor-based calibration, to enable camera-based tracking. Therefore, they are not portable and unavailable for any open-source editing to fit the needs of other medical simulations.

Overall, optical based tracking framework requires either multiple cameras or involves other sensor devices to improve the tracking accuracy. To our best knowledge, a single camera based optical tracking framework that supports open-source development of medical simulation does not exist.

III. METHOD

Our method used portable devices and open-source CVT. Any simulation prototype can adopt the approach. In this section, we will detail our approach in terms of experiment setup, including adopted devices, a unique marker design, and the implementation of the OpenCV tracking software.

A. Experiment Setup

Figure 1. Experiment Setup: 1) Phantom; 2) Cubic Shape Marker Attached to A Mock Transducer; 3) Camera; 4) Laptop.

The proposed method in this study used four pieces of equipment to develop a running prototype, as seen in Figure 1:

1) An upper body mannequin as a phantom
2) Four chessboard markers glued to a cubic shape cardboard and attached to the top of a mock transducer
3) A Logitech web camera (hidden behind of the laptop) with a resolution of 720p/30fps
4) A Lenovo laptop with AMD Ryzen 7 5700u CPU, AMD Radeon Graphics, and 40 GB memory to run the OpenCV method for computer vision-based tracking

B. *Tracking Method*

Our tracking method used OpenCV [16], an open-source computer vision library. The original OpenCV program was designed to use several cameras from different angles to track a single marker. The setting can easily capture the translation and rotation of a marker based on streaming tracking of all cameras. However, in order to provide a portable framework, we only adopted one camera and designed a cubic-shape marker box in our setting.

1) *Marker*

The cubic-shaped box consists of four markers glued on the four sides (left, right, front, and back) of a box, as seen in Figure 1 (2). This unique marker design can accommodate the development of a portable system. Each marker is measured as 4 by 3 in terms of the number of Internal Corner Points (ICP), points where the black square corners connecting with each other [17]. This size is cropped from the original marker measured 9 by 4 ICP in order to fit a hand-held medical device. Figure 2 shows the comparison of the two-marker sizes.

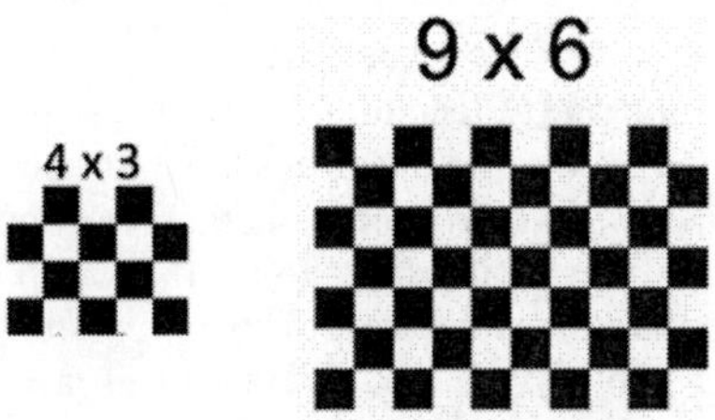

(a) (b)

Figure 2. Markers a) size 4x3; b) size 9x6

OpenCV is designed for multiple tracking of several cameras. Therefore, many sample programs consist of multiple streaming tracking. Figure 3 shows the top view (xz-plane) of two experiment settings. The camera lens is directly facing the xy-plane. The y coordinate is perpendicular to the xz plane. As seen in Figure 3 (a), two cameras placed diagonally (45-degree angle) facing against a marker can easily monitor the rotation of the marker along the y coordinate. The marker can rotate 90 degrees to the left or right, while cameras take turns to track the rotation when the marker is no longer seen by one camera in a 180-degree tracking angle. However, two camera-based tracking would be inconvenient for a portable system design. After all, we came up with the design of the box shape marker, which allows us to track the rotation of a marker easily when there is only one camera tracking the marker at a limited tracking angle. For example, as seen in Figure 3(b), when the front marker is rotating to the left along the y coordinate at approximately 45 degrees, it starts to lose the tracking of the camera since its chessboard is no longer seen by the camera lens. However, at this point, the right-side marker on the box becomes available for camera detection, which is rotating toward the camera with a less than 45-degree angle. The system would then add a 90-degree angle change to the rotation vector as a subtraction factor. This solution permits single-camera tracking while producing a fast and accurate rotation vector for the study. Similarly, when tracking the markers glued on the top and bottom of the box, the system can easily monitor the rotation along the x coordinate.

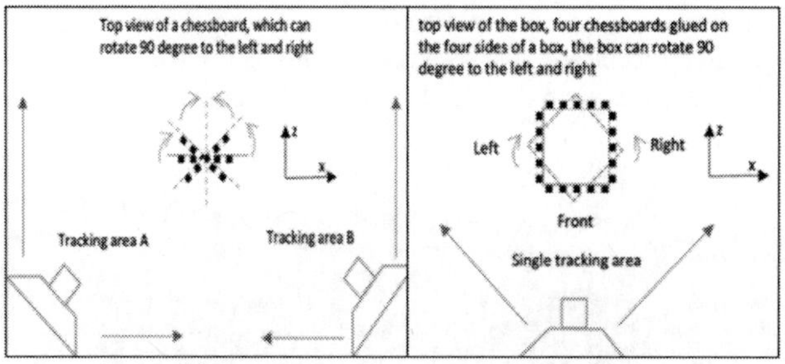

(a) (b)

Figure 3. (a) Multiple camera and one marker tracking (b) One camera and box shape marker-based tracking

Figure 4 presents the real case scenarios for our experiment. The camera is facing the front marker initially. When a subject was rotating the marker along the y coordinate (perpendicular to the mannequin's face) to the left side of the marker, the right side marker became available for tracking. At this time, we will update the subtraction factor to indicate the rotation angle of -90 degrees.

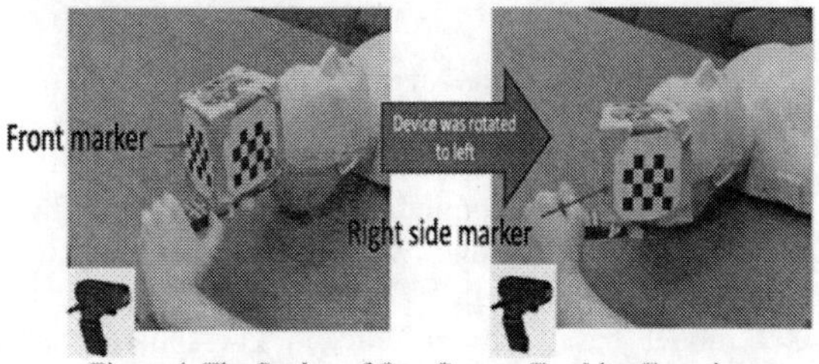

Figure 4. The Setting of One Camera Tracking Experiment

2) *Tracking Framework*

Figure 5 presents the system diagram of the implemented tracking software using OpenCV. The framework system started with camera-based calibration to learn the orientation of the phantom. The marker was then converted to a grayscale image for chessboard recognition using the method findChessBoardCorners(). We adopted three flags in this method call: 1) threshold to convert the image to black and white only, 2) normalize the gamma of the image in order to find the chessboard easier, and 3) add a fast check that speeds up the chessboard detection process. If a chessboard is detected, the findChessBoardCorners() method searches 6 ICPs during the stream tracking. Once the 6 ICPs were found, they went through the cornerSubPix() method to return a more accurate ICP measurement using the image gradient described in Forstner's method [18]. Afterward, the calibrateCamera() method runs the solvePnP algorithm, which will estimate the marker's pose using the 6 processed ICPs and their corresponding image projection points. The algorithm runs Levenberg-Marquardt optimization [19] iteratively, which helps to calculate such a pose by minimizing the reprojection error. This approach will finalize the pose by generating the translation and rotation vectors. Meanwhile, our script checks the rotation vector along the y coordinate to update the subtraction factor. The framework produces a translation vector, a rotation vector, and a subtraction factor. These three outputs can be used by any simulation system that needs a tracking feature.

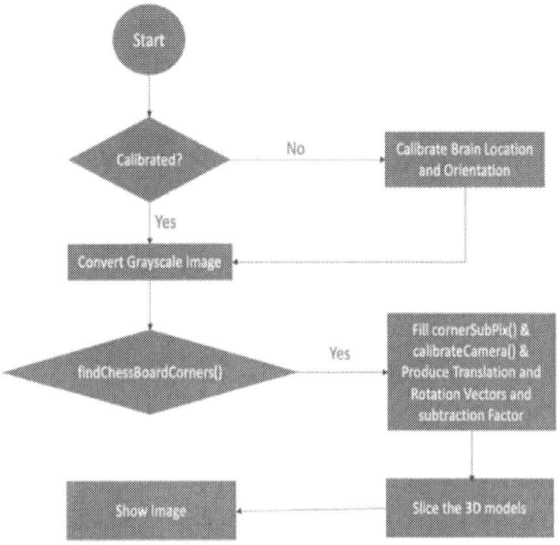

Figure 5. OpenCV Program Diagram

IV. A Case Study

The framework was applied to a simulated cranial (head) ultrasound to verify its usage. We adopted a 3D brain mesh model from PyVista [20] in VTK format. To properly slice the 3D model based on the tracked chessboard that is orthogonal to the slice, the ManySlicesAlongPoints() method [21] from PyVista was used. We used the translation vector [X_t, Y_t, Z_t] and rotation vector [X_r, Y_r, Z_r] obtained from the OpenCV tracking program to calculate a required path [X, Y] as shown below:

$$X = (\tan\left((X_r - 90)\frac{\pi}{180}\right) \times Y) + X_t;$$

$$Y = \text{points: } 0 - 216;$$

Then, the SliceAlongManyPoint() method produced a line/path based on the calculated [X, Y] and sliced the 3D brain model that is perpendicular to the path. As seen in Figure 4, the face of a mock transducer, facing against the top head of the mannequin, is orthogonal to the marker planes on all four sides. Therefore, an orthogonal slice is the proper setting for our experimental setup.

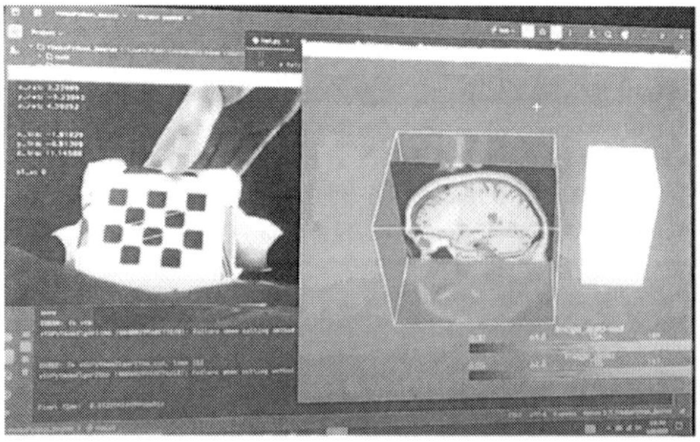
Figure 6. A prototype for a simulated cranial ultrasound

In Figure 6, the simulated ultrasound prototype presents three windows side by side. The top left window showed the real-time tracking of the box marker by highlighting the tracked marker; the bottom left window displayed the running script of the program by outputting both translation and rotation vectors; the top right window produced a slice of the 3D brain model for the simulated cranial ultrasound based on the location and orientation of the mock transducer/box marker. A white cubic on the right side of this output window indicates the box marker's corresponding position toward the calibrated brain in virtual space. Note that our prototype has not yet presented its form in ultrasound texture due to time constraints; however, our previous ultrasound image simulation techniques [22] can be easily adopted by the platform to fulfill the case study of the simulation. Nevertheless, the presented outcome does not impact our research goal for a tracking framework based on CVT to support medical simulation.

V. Results

The proposed tracking framework can produce real-time tracking based on our simulated cranial ultrasound experiments. The adopted devices work well to support the newly developed tracking technique. The simulated ultrasound is presented instantly at a 30 FPS rate according to the movement of the mock transducer. The rotation was captured accurately at 90 degrees to the left and right along the y coordinate using the subtraction factor.

The dual windows design (tracked marker and simulation production), as seen in Figure 6, enables us to explore the tracking space fully. The showing of the mock transducer in the top right window presents the true location of the device in the physical world. The tracked marker reflected the rotation angle. The script is running effectively to support the movement of the transducer. The most important evaluation is that the generated cranial ultrasound slice reflects the accurate orientation and translation of the brain model in the phantom

The simulation framework can be easily adopted by any simulation research. We plan to release the software as a free resource for academic usages.

VI. Conclusion

The proposed framework developed an innovative approach to track a box shape marker in order to build a portable tracking system using one web camera. The system can be used by any simulation-related prototype, providing conveniences to medical students who can practice training in any setting without labs. The case study presented an ultrasound simulation setting, which has approved the effectiveness of the framework that offers real-time stream tracking. Although the simulation prototype is not ready for ultrasound training, the presented prototype provides us with a way to evaluate the framework regarding tracking accuracy.

The framework can be adopted by any simulation research to monitor the orientation and rotation of a movable medical device. It is particularly useful to augment a virtual object based on the movement of a physical object in any domain setting.

Acknowledgment

We would like to thank US Department of Education for GAANN award #P200A190033 to support this research work.

References

[1] A. Nahum. *Patient Safety Representatives Unite to Implement Global Patient Safety Action Plan in the United States*. Centers for Disease Control and Prevention, City, 2021.

[2] T. Blum, A. Rieger, N. Navab, H. Friess and M. Martignoni. "A Review of Computer-Based Simulators for Ultrasound Training". *Simulation in Healthcare*, vol 8, no. 2, pp. 98-108, 2013.

[3] Schallware *Schallware Ulrasound Simulator*. Schallware, City, 2024.

[4] SurgicalScience *Ultrasound Mentor Platforms*. Surgical Science, City, 2024.

[5] Menache, A. *1 - Motion Capture Primer*. Morgan Kaufmann, City, 2011.

[6] Intelligent Ultrasound *ScanTrainer: Simulation in Transvaginal and Transabdomnial Ultrasound*. Intelligent Ultrasound, City, 2024.

[7] SurgicalScience *VR add on for ultrasound mentor*. Surgical Science, City, 2024.

[8] D. Markov-Vetter, J. Muehl, D. Schmalstieg, E. Sorantin and M. Riccabona. "3D augmented reality simulator for neonatal cranial sonography". *Comput Assist Radiol Surg*, vol. 1230, pp. 483-487, 2001.

[9] Z. Duan, Z. Yuan, X. Liao, W. Si and J. Zhao. "3D tracking and positioning of surgical instruments in virtual surgery simulation". *Journal of multimedia*, vol. 6, no. 6 2011.

[10] NaturalPoint Inc. *OptiTrack*. NaturalPoint Inc., City, 2024.

[11] T. Ameler, K. Blohme, L. Brandt, R. Brüngel, A. Hensel, L. Huber, F. Kuper, J. Swoboda, M. Warnecke and M. Warzecha. "*A comparative evaluation of steamvr tracking and the optitrack system for medical device tracking*". IEEE, City, 2019.

[12] Medge Platforms Inc. *Volutracer O.P.U.S.: Optical Positiong Ultrasound Simulator*. Medge Platforms, Inc, City, 2023.

[13] S. Lee, H. Lee, H. Choi, S. Jeon and J. Hong. "Effective calibration of an endoscope to an optical tracking system for medical augmented reality". *Cogent Engineering*, vol. 4, no. 1, pp. 1359955, 2017.

[14] Northern Digital Inc. *Optical Navigation*. NDI, City, 2022.

[15] Advanced Real Time Tracking GmbH & Co. KG *CAPTA Tracking technolgy*. Advanced Realtime Tracking, City, 2024.

[16] OpenCV *Open Source Computer Vision: OpenCV modules*. OpenCV, City, 2024.

[17] OpenCV *findChessboardCorners(): OpenCV Document*. OpenCV, City, 2024.

[18] OpenCV *cornerSubPix(): OpenCV Document*. City, 2024.

[19] OpenCV *Perspective-N-Point Pose (PnP) Computation: OpenCV Doc*. City, 2024.

[20] PyVista *PyVista: 3D plotting and mesh analysis through a streamlined interface for the Visualization Toolkit (VTK)*. The PyVista Developers, City, 2023.

[21] B. Sullivan. *Many Slices Along Points - PVGeo Documentation*. GenDocs, City, 2020.

[22] B. Sun. and F. McKenzie. "Real-time sonography simulation for medical training". *International journal of education and information technologies*, vol 5, no. 3, pp. 328-335, 2011.

Simulating Olson's Bandits: An ABM Exploration of Government Decision Dynamics

Chasen Jeffries
School of Social Science, Policy & Evaluation
Claremont Graduate University
Claremont, United States of America
email: chasen.jeffries@cgu.edu

Abstract— **This study employs agent-based modeling (ABM) to simulate Mancur Olson's theory of roving and stationary bandits, with a focus on governance and economic performance. While empirical research has investigated Olson's theory, real-world case studies have not provided the best natural experiments to thoroughly examine it. This research investigates how bandits, under varying initial conditions, parameter values, and environments, govern and maximize their gains. The model, tested through scenario analysis, finds that stationary bandits consistently perform strongly due to their ability to invest in their subjects, giving them a long-term advantage. In contrast, roving bandits exhibit less stability, with varying conditions determining whether they survive, die out, or transition to stationary bandits. Those that transition manage to survive and thrive without investing in their subjects, challenging Olson's assumption that public goods beyond peace and order are essential for societal stability. While these initial results require further validation, they may offer future insights into governance in contexts of weak state capacity.**

Keywords-Agent-Based Modeling (ABM); Olson's Bandits; Complex Adaptive System; Co-Evolution; Government Formation; Decision Dynamics.

I. INTRODUCTION

In 1993, Mancur Olson published a paper exploring how bandits could explain variations in governance and economic performance outcomes [12]. Olson posited that roving and stationary bandits are rational agents trying to maximize their gains. He demonstrated how their endowed characteristics and operational context simultaneously reveal the formation of governments and the nature of their decisions. These heterogenous bandits dynamically adapt within complex adaptive systems and co-evolve with their subjects to maximize their fitness function. Over the ensuing decades, scholars have extensively critiqued and engaged in debates spurred by this theory, focusing on the origins and fundamental elements influencing governance.

Building upon Olson's foundational work, subsequent researchers [10][13][19] have further developed the initial theory. These scholarly contributions aim to more precisely articulate the dynamics between rulers and the ruled, as well as the evolution from banditry to established governance and the provisioning of public goods. In 1997, Banks, Olson, and Porter [2] developed an experimental model to investigate how agents' decision-making processes vary with their time horizons and levels of risk aversion. While empirical studies have attempted to explore Olson's theory using natural experiments, these case studies often face limitations due to the gap between theoretical conditions and the real-world cases. This misalignment constrains the ability of researchers to fully test and validate the theory.

We extend the established literature by simulating Olson's concepts of roving and stationary bandits, aiming to assess whether theoretical predictions align with our simulation outcomes. This simulation provides an experimental framework that enables empirical investigation of government decision-making dynamics in ways that real-world natural experiments cannot. In our simulations, roving and stationary bandits compete within a dynamic environment, allowing us to examine the co-evolution of heterogeneous bandit decision-making with their subjects and its impact on macroeconomic outcomes. Our model incorporates a complex adaptive system that facilitates feedback mechanisms, enabling the bandits and subjects to dynamically evolve in pursuit of optimizing their strategic outcomes. This model represents an initial effort to rigorously evaluate Olson's core principles, particularly focusing on the effects of government-subject relationships and government decision-making processes on economic performance.

This research offers significant practical implications, as our simulations underscore the profound impact of government-subject dynamics and decision-making processes on economic outcomes, suggesting avenues for policy intervention and governance reform. Moreover, our model delineates specific scenarios and conditions under which governments emerge and evolve, offering insights into the transition points at which roving bandits opt to become stationary, thus stabilizing their governance.

This model represents a pioneering effort to simulate the dynamic co-evolution of rulers and ruled, unraveling the complexities of ruler decision-making and its impact on the economic performance of both governments and subjects. Central to our model is Olson's insight that rational roving bandits may elect to become stationary to optimize their fitness function, engendering a symbiotic co-evolution with their subjects. Furthermore, our simulations explore how foundational government decisions, such as taxation and investment, influenced by local environmental dynamics, result in varied outcomes across generations. However, this model does not address the potential transition to democracy or the problematic tendencies inherent in autocratic successions.

This paper is structured in the following format. First, we review the empirical paradigm to frame the research in context. Next, we present a detailed overview of the agent-based model articulating the different agents and their capabilities. Third, we explore the model through baseline and scenario analyses to identify initial results. Finally, we articulate the conclusions and outline the next steps for future research to build upon.

II. Related Works

To contextualize the problem, we review the literature on both Olson's theory and agent-based modeling (ABM) to illustrate the challenges faced by previous research and the benefits provided by agent-based simulations.

A. *Olson's Bandits and Government-Subject Dynamics*

In his 1993 theory [12], Olson posited that within a competitive landscape of roving bandits, rational actors would opt to become stationary bandits, recognizing the potential for greater wealth accumulation as autocrats compared to the transient gains from roving banditry. Stationary bandits impose lower taxes than their roving counterparts and establish a peace and order, as well as contributing to the provision of public goods. This arrangement incentivizes subjects to invest in the future, promising them greater long-term rewards under a new equilibrium where both parties benefit from a symbiotic relationship. Thus, Olson's theory offers a pivotal explanation for government formation, addressing and overcoming the fundamental issue of collective action problems, and governance impact on economic development.

Following Olson's seminal postulation, numerous scholars have expanded upon his theoretical framework [8][19], delving into the nuanced decision-making of rulers and their balancing act between extracting resources from society and providing public goods [7][10][13]. Alternatively, Moselle and Polak [11] present a critical viewpoint, arguing that the provision of public goods by rulers, while potentially enhancing economic performance, may not necessarily translate to better outcomes for subjects. While these models elucidate theoretical principles, they often fall short in empirical testing. Addressing this gap, Banks, Olson, and Porter [2] developed an experimental model to investigate the decision making postulated by Olson, offering empirical support to his theoretical assertions. While this model tests key elements of Olson's theory, our research goes a step further by rigorously examining the intricate dynamics between rulers and subjects within a constantly evolving landscape of roving and stationary bandits.

Empirical research has investigated Olson's theory using natural experiments, yielding some valuable insights. However, these studies often face challenges in aligning real-world cases with the theoretical constructs, as the complexities of natural settings frequently deviate from the controlled assumptions of the theory. As a result, the empirical evidence supporting Olson's framework remains incomplete.

B. *Simulating Dyadic Decision Making in Evolving Landscapes*

Recent decades have witnessed a significant paradigm shift in social sciences through the proliferation of agent-based simulations, facilitating bottom-up analyses. The 1996 release of "Growing Artificial Societies" by Epstein & Axtell [4] showcased the profound potential of simple, iteratively modified models to yield insightful and paradigm-shifting results. In their simulation, heterogeneous agents, with distinct endowments of skill and resources engage, in competition within a dynamic landscape to secure resources. This model laid significant groundwork for employing agent-based modeling in simulating complex social science processes, opening new avenues for research and theory development.

Researchers have utilized this technique to model key scenarios and theories, contributing to empirical research by creating heterogeneous agents endowed with specific capabilities and initial conditions, which adapt within a dynamic, uncertain landscape to maximize their fitness functions [1][15][18]. The Wolf-Sheep predation model, significantly explored in studies by Wilensky et al. [16] [17], Marucco et al. [9], and Husnain [6], simulates the evolution of population dynamics based on simple decision-making within a dynamic landscape, offering insights into the dynamic co-evolution of species and the sensitive dependence on initial conditions.

The foundational simulations in the field provide a rich background that underpins our simulation efforts. Our bandit-subject relationship's population dynamics parallel those observed in the wolf-sheep predation model [6][16][17]. We also adopt Epstein and Axtell's [4] simple observation and decision-making rules to construct the decision tree for our roving bandits. Lastly, by incorporating Olson's core decision-making dynamics through a simplified set of rules and equations, we effectively simulate the evolving landscape and the behavior of self-maximizing bandits as theorized by Olson.

Social science simulations offer a controlled environment where researchers can systematically model complex phenomena, such as government decision-making, allowing for a level of precision and experimentation that is not feasible in real-world settings. These simulations enable the exploration of theoretical scenarios in ways that natural experiments cannot.

By integrating both empirical insights from natural experiments and the rigorous control provided by agent-based simulations, this study bridges the gap between theoretical predictions and real-world complexities, offering a more comprehensive understanding of Olson's bandit theory in evolving governance structures.

III. Modeling Olsons Bandits

To support reproducibility and demonstrate validity, we outline the fundamental components of our ABM simulating

Olson's bandits, explaining the key assumptions, characteristics, and decision-making elements.

A. *Bandit Decision Making*

Figure 1 presents a detailed overview of the capabilities and decision-making methods of our heterogeneous bandits, highlighting their distinct strategies. We begin with the assumption that bandit fitness—defined as the change in a bandit's resources—is the most effective indicator of success. This assumption is rooted in Olson's theory, where bandits, or government agents, are rational and self-maximizing actors who prioritize their own well-being. Although both types of bandits possess the ability to tax their subjects, they are distinguished by unique capabilities that allow for a broad exploration of behaviors. Roving bandits, represented in blue, utilize a decision tree to strategically determine their movements. In contrast, stationary bandits, depicted in red, can invest in their territories to offer public goods beyond mere peace, enhancing the well-being of their subjects.

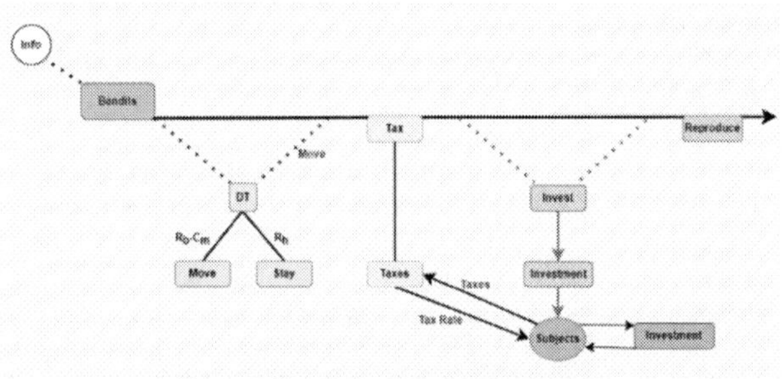

Figure 1: Bandit Decision Making Model

B. *Movement*

Initially, both types of bandits assess the local environment, gathering information on available resources to inform their strategies. Utilizing this information, roving bandits determine the optimal location for their next move, integrating this into their decision tree. The best location is characterized by the most abundant resources and the absence of stationary bandit control. Having assessed the optimal move and its associated costs, roving bandits consult their decision tree to choose between moving or remaining at their current position. Should multiple roving bandits converge on the same location, a conflict ensues, resulting in all but one bandit flee to a randomly selected nearby space.

C. *Taxation*

Following the conclusion of all movements, both roving and stationary bandits levy taxes on their subjects at predetermined rates, subsequently collecting the resulting income. The imposed tax rate directly influences the subjects' investment rate, dictating the proportion of their resources they allocate to development. In this model, the subjects' investment rate inversely correlates with rate at which they are taxed, reflecting the delicate balance that stationary bandits must navigate between taxation and potential returns on investment. Rooted in Olson's core assumption, our model posits that subjects are motivated to invest in their domains primarily when they are assured a share of the investment's returns. Subjects' investment rates are calculated using the following equation:

$$I_s = 1 - T_b - 0.4 \qquad (1)$$

Is represents the investment rate of the subject, and Tb denotes the tax rate imposed by the bandit.

We establish a base saving rate of 0.4, representing the minimum threshold that subjects must achieve before considering future investments. In scenarios where taxation is absent, the investment rate gradually increases, reflecting the subjects' growing optimism about future prospects. Thus, the interplay between the base rate and taxation critically influences the subjects' willingness to invest.

D. *Investment*

Subsequently, stationary bandits invest in their subjects. This action embodies Olson's fundamental assumption: for society to thrive, governments must ensure peace, property rights, and contract enforcement. Although our published results utilize a simple interest equation, the model is also compatible with compound and exponential interest calculations. The simple interest calculation involves the bandits' investment amount (Ib), their investment time horizon (Hb), and an assumed interest rate of 0.05.

$$Y = I_b * r * H_b \qquad (2)$$

Once stationary bandits have invested in their subjects, they are precluded from making further investments until the initial investment has matured. Subjects have the ability to invest in themselves by applying their investment rate, as determined by (1), to the simple interest formula.

At the end of each tick in the simulation, bandits undergo base attrition, reflecting the necessity to sustain themselves to avoid extinction. Wealthy bandits, having sufficiently accumulated resources, possess the ability to reproduce, thereby generating new bandits of their respective type—either roving or stationary.

Validating this model poses challenges due to the lack of directly comparable real-world data. Therefore, we employ face validity, ensuring that the model's behavior aligns with the theoretical expectations of Olson's bandit theory. Specifically, we assess whether the decision-making processes and outcomes in the simulation are consistent with the core principles of rational, self-maximizing agents and the dynamics observed in other related theoretical work. This approach provides a foundational level of validation, though future work could explore additional validation techniques as more empirical data becomes available.

IV. RESULTS

Here we analyze the model's performance across different scenarios, evaluating how roving and stationary bandits behave under a range of initial conditions, parameter settings, and environmental contexts.

A. *Baseline*

To begin, we establish a benchmark to gauge the baseline performance of bandits within the simulation, serving as a foundational comparison point for assessing outcomes across various scenarios. Based on initial testing to explore the performance of the model under a variety of initial conditions and parameter values, we established two key conclusions. First, we set the model to stop after 250 ticks, during which time the system undergoes phase shifts and unstable equilibrium changes before reaching a stable state. This duration allows us to capture both short-term and long-term dynamics. Second, we identified key variables that significantly impact model performance, which led us to fix certain parameters (e.g., population) while varying others (e.g., tax rate) to better understand their effects. Table 1 outlines the values of key variables, including bandits' operational parameters and subjects' behavioral tendencies, essential for understanding the simulation dynamics. Normal distributions are applied to model variables such as the bandits' observation range, tax rate, investment rate, investment time, and the subjects' optimism, ensuring variation in these parameters. This approach creates a dynamic and realistic simulation landscape, presenting bandits and subjects with a nuanced environment characterized by variable costs and opportunities.

TABLE 1. BASELINE INITIAL CONDITIONS AND PARAMETER VALUES

Parameters	*Description*	*Base value*
Population	Total number of Bandits	50
Stationary Population	The initial number of stationary Bandits	25
Observation Range	How far the Bandits can see around them (mean & standard deviation)	3:1.5
Move Cost	The cost for Bandits to move one step.	2
Spawn Rate	The rate new Bandits spawn from the fit bandits	1
Attrition Rate	The rate Bandits lose wealth each tick	0.25
Tax Rate	The Bandits tax rate for their subjects	0.4:0.2
Investment Rate	The Stationary Bandit investment rate into their subjects	0.25:0.125
Investment Time	The Stationary Bandit time of investments	1.5:0.75
Optimism	The Optimism of subjects that the future will get better.	0.025:0.012

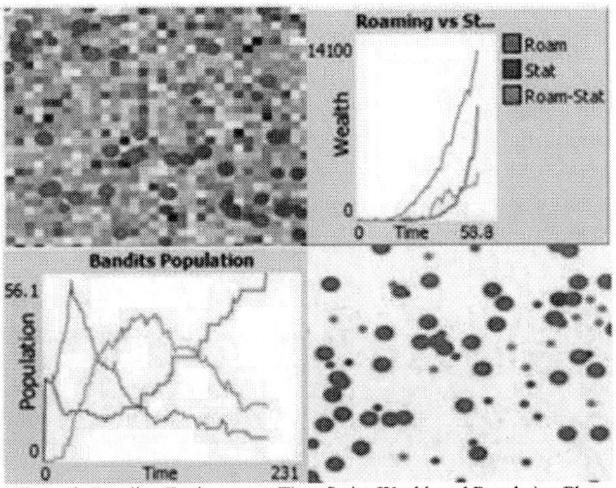

Figure 2: Baseline Environment, Time Series Wealth and Population Plots

In the baseline scenario, visualized in Figure 2, roving bandits initially outperform stationary bandits, swiftly accumulating resources and expanding in population as illustrated by the first 25 ticks on the time series wealth plot. However, this dominance is short-lived; stationary bandits gradually surpass roving bandits as their investments mature. The intensifying competition among roving bandits diminishes their returns significantly, especially as available subjects become scarce and less inclined to invest in themselves due to frequent raids. Consequently, the landscape undergoes a dramatic transformation, from a normal distribution, resource-rich environment to one starkly barren except for the wealth now concentrated within the domains of stationary bandits.

Interestingly, the simulation reveals a bifurcation among roving bandits driven by their tax rate, leading to distinct paths in their evolution. Roving bandits that adopt lower tax rates transition to roving-stationary status, signified by turning orange, after remaining immobile for 10 consecutive ticks. These newly stationary bandits often outnumber their roving counterparts and maintain their fitness by assuming a leadership role over their subjects, taxing them minimally without offering public goods. This minimal taxation strategy ensures that their subjects remain incentivized to invest, showcasing how rational bandits sustain their autocratic position without providing public goods, demonstrating a new equilibrium strategy. In contrast, true roving bandits, maintaining their nomadic nature, levy nearly maximum taxation rates above 90 percent.

Ultimately, true stationary bandits—those who are both capable and willing to invest in their subjects—outperform both roving bandits and converted stationary bandits. This outcome provides strong empirical support for Olson's theory, illustrating that rational bandits opt for a stationary lifestyle and, by investing in their subjects, achieve superior long-term performance compared to their counterparts.

B. Resource Rich Environment

In this scenario illustrated in Figure 3, we introduce our bandits to a resource-rich environment. The primary objective is to examine the evolution of roving bandits' decision-making processes in response to an environment abundant in resources from the outset. Additionally, this scenario investigates whether a higher resource starting environment empowers stationary bandits to further dominate the landscape and outperform their roving counterparts.

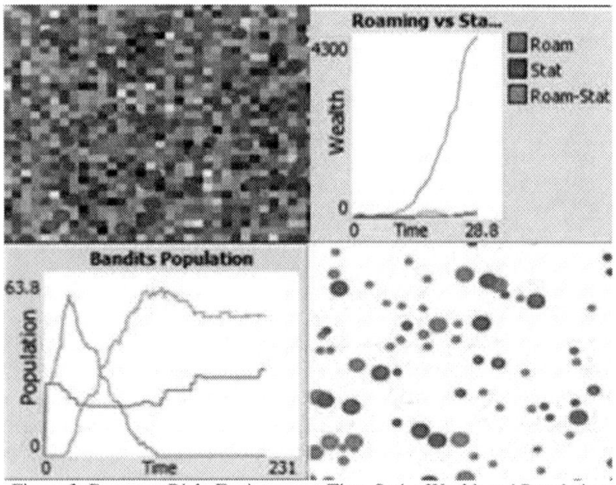

Figure 3: Resource Rich Environment, Time Series Wealth and Population Plots

The bandit population time series plot reveals that roving bandits almost invariably face extinction. Further investigation reveals a significant population explosion among roving bandits, exacerbating the competition for resources. This intense competition for an initially abundant resource pool rapidly depletes the landscape, precipitating a population collapse reminiscent of dynamics observed in Wolf-Sheep predation models.

Roving bandits that strategically transition to stationary status often become the most populous agents. This suggests that, in the medium term, transitioning roving bandits capture more resources and exhibit superior fitness, resulting in faster population growth compared to original stationary bandits. Both transitioning roving bandits and original stationary bandits reach an equilibrium stabilizing of their populations. Despite population stability, original stationary bandits maintain a long-term advantage over their transitioning counterparts, attributed to their investments in public goods that bolster the economic performance of their subjects.

C. *Resource Rich and Low Tax Environment*

Figure 4 shows this how we expand on scenario one's resource-rich landscape, this evolution introduces lower tax rates for bandits, now ranging from 0 to 0.4, a reduction from the original range of 0 to 0.8. This adjustment aims to more precisely assess the tax rate's influence on both roving and stationary bandits' strategies and outcomes. The key questions are whether lower tax rates disproportionately impact roving bandits over stationary ones, and if such rates enable roving bandits to secure gains without deterring subjects' investments—thereby maintaining a fertile landscape and averting the population bubble and collapse observed previously.

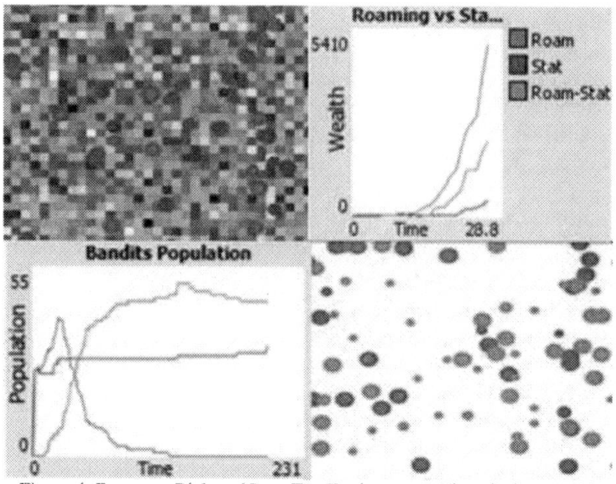

Figure 4: Resource Rich and Low Tax Environment, Time Series Wealth and Population Plots

Roving bandits face rapid decline; however, the majority transition to stationary status, adopting it as the dominant strategy for survival. This adaptation underscores an equilibrium where low tax rates enable former roving bandits to not only survive but thrive, effectively becoming successful roving-stationary bandits.

Stationary bandits that invest in their subjects maintain the upper hand in the model, excelling in resource capture through their strategic investments. The mutual benefits arising from bandits' investments and subjects' self-investment create a symbiotic relationship, enabling both parties to thrive. Roving-Stationary bandits adopt a nuanced strategy, levying lower taxes to incentivize subjects' self-investment, thereby benefiting from a more laissez-faire approach

D. *Resource Rich and High Tax Environment*

Figure 5 examines the impact of high taxes on governance decision-making, contrasting with Scenario 2's focus on low taxes. This scenario aims to further unravel the dynamic equilibria among roving, roving-stationary, and stationary bandits, dictated by their differing tax strategies. Here bandits are given high tax rates ranging from 0.2 to 1, a significant increase from Scenario 2's 0 to 0.5 range and the baseline's 0 to 0.8.

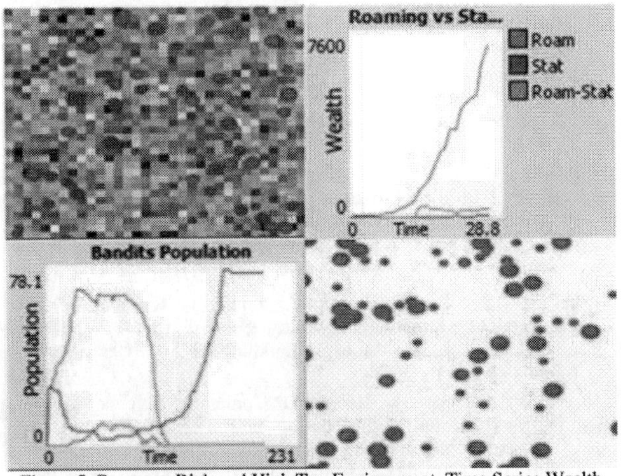

Figure 5: Resource Rich and High Tax Environment, Time Series Wealth and Population Plots

Stationary bandits subject to high tax rates face rapid extinction, while those imposing low to medium tax rates not only survive but flourish. Likewise, roving-stationary bandits only survive under low tax rates, mirroring the survival condition of their stationary counterparts.

Initially, roving bandits seem to adopt the dominant strategy, with very few opting to transition into a roving-stationary status. The roving bandits' population experiences growth, stabilizes for a brief period, and then undergoes a sudden collapse. Ultimately, this scenario proves unsustainable for roving bandits, leading to their complete extinction.

E. *Comparison of Scenario Performances*

In this section, we systematically compare the performance of bandits across the scenarios to highlight key differences and similarities in behavior and outcomes. Despite being an initial exploration of Olson's bandits with a relatively simple ruleset, our simulation yields significant conclusions. Firstly, rational roving bandits strategically adapt to their environments by transitioning into stationary bandits. Secondly, despite their adaptation, these roving-stationary bandits abstain from providing public goods or making investments in their subjects. This reveals a previously unidentified equilibrium for autocrats, challenging Olson's assumption that societal thriving requires both peace and public goods. Thirdly, although roving-stationary bandits find a niche to survive and flourish, stationary bandits offering additional public goods emerge as the model's fittest agents, in alignment with Olson's theory.

Across all scenarios, roving bandits are significantly affected by changes in initial conditions, parameters values, and environment. Their survivability is highly contingent on favorable conditions. In certain contexts, roving bandits experience strong initial performance, leading to a population explosion. However, this rapid growth depletes local resources, often resulting in an eventual extinction event, mimicking patterns observed in predator-prey models. Under less favorable conditions, a bifurcation occurs where roving bandits with lower tax rates are able to successfully transition into roving-stationary bandits, adopting a more sustainable strategy.

In contrast, stationary bandits exhibit more stable performance across a wide range of conditions. Whether in low-resource or high-resource environments, and regardless of tax rates, stationary bandits manage to survive and eventually thrive. Their ability to invest in their local environment provides them with a significant long-term advantage. However, under extreme conditions—such as high tax rates—stationary bandits can face early extinction if their investments do not mature in time.

For both roving and stationary bandits, excessively high taxes appear to be a burden rather than a benefit. While high taxes can support long-term performance if the bandits survive the initial phases, they often lead to early decline. Overall, the key patterns across scenarios suggest that resource availability and taxation strategies are critical determinants of bandit survival and success.

V. CONCLUSIONS

This study contributes to the literature by providing a systematic agent-based simulation of Olson's bandit theory, revealing how varying conditions affect the evolution of governance structures. Unlike empirical studies constrained by real-world complexities, this simulation allows for controlled exploration of bandit decision-making dynamics across a variety of scenarios. Our findings both support and challenge aspects of Olson's theory.

The strong performance of stationary bandits investing in their subjects aligns with Olson's theory. However, the actions of roving bandits suggest that the pathway from banditry to stable governance may not always require heavy investment in public goods. Several scenarios illustrated that bandits can thrive without investing in their subjects, revealing this new equilibrium. This challenges the assumption that provision of additional public goods, beyond peace, is essential for societal stability. While we hold back from drawing definitive practical implications until the model can be further validated, the initial results indicate potential relevance for situations characterized by weak state capacity.

Future models can build on these foundations and improve alignment with Olson's theory by incorporating learning mechanics that enable bandits to adapt, optimizing their tax and investment strategies. Moreover, stronger calibration and validation with real-world data can enhance its accuracy and practical relevance.

REFERENCES

[1] R. L. Axtell, et al. "Population growth and collapse in a multiagent model of the Kayenta Anasazi in Long House Valley," Proc. Natl. Acad. Sci., vol. 99, suppl_3, pp. 7275-7279, Apr. 2002. https://doi.org/10.1073/pnas.092080799

[2] J. Banks, M. Olson, and D. Porter, "An Experimental Analysis of the Bandit Problem," Economic Theory, vol. 10, no. 1, pp. 55–77, 1997. http://www.jstor.org/stable/25055024. Retrieved: Sept. 2024.

[3] E. D. Bó, P. Hernández, and S. Mazzuca, "The paradox of civilization: Pre-institutional sources of security and

prosperity," NBER Working Paper, 2015. http://www.nber.org/papers/w21829. Retrieved: Sept. 2024.

[4] J. M. Epstein and R. Axtell, Growing Artificial Societies: Social Science from the Bottom Up. Brookings Institution Press, 1996.

[5] R. Höijer, "Theft by Bandits and Taxation by Kings: A Critique of Mancur Olson on State-Formation," Political Studies Review, vol. 2, pp. 24-38, 2004. https://doi.org/10.1111/j.1478-9299.2004.00002.x. Retrieved: Sept. 2024.

[6] M. Husnain and N. Shafi, "An extension to wolf sheep predation (docked hybrid) agent-based model in NetLogo," Journal of Software Engineering & Intelligent Systems, vol. 6, no. 1, pp 42-46, 2021.

[7] R. Kirstein and S. Voigt, "The Violent and the Weak: When Dictators Care about Social Contracts," The American Journal of Economics and Sociology, vol. 65, no. 4, pp. 863–890, 2006. http://www.jstor.org/stable/27739596. Retrieved: Sept. 2024.

[8] P. Kurrild-Klitgaard and G. Tinggaard Svendsen, "Rational Bandits: Plunder, Public Goods, and the Vikings," Public Choice, vol. 117, pp. 255–272, 2003. https://doi.org/10.1023/B:PUCH.0000003733.81946.d3. Retrieved: Sept. 2024.

[9] F. Marucco and E. J. B. McIntire, "Predicting spatio-temporal recolonization of large carnivore populations and livestock depredation risk: wolves in the Italian Alps," Journal of Applied Ecology, vol. 47, no. 4, pp. 789–798, 2010. http://www.jstor.org/stable/40835697. Retrieved: Sept. 2024.

[10] M. C. McGuire and M. Olson, "The Economics of Autocracy and Majority Rule: The Invisible Hand and the Use of Force," Journal of Economic Literature, vol. 34, no. 1, pp. 72–96, 1996. http://www.jstor.org/stable/2729410. Retrieved: Sept. 2024.

[11] B. Moselle and B. Polak, "A Model of a Predatory State," Journal of Law, Economics, & Organization, vol. 17, no. 1, pp. 1–33, 2001. http://www.jstor.org/stable/3554995. Retrieved: Sept. 2024.

[12] M. Olson, "Dictatorship, Democracy, and Development," The American Political Science Review, vol. 87, no. 3, pp. 567–576, 1993. https://doi.org/10.2307/2938736. Retrieved: Sept. 2024.

[13] E. E. Piano, "State capacity and public choice: a critical survey," Public Choice, vol. 178, no. 1/2, pp. 289–309, 2019. https://www.jstor.org/stable/48703356. Retrieved: Sept. 2024.

[14] T. Sandler and J. Tschirhart, "Club theory: thirty years later," Public Choice, vol. 93, pp. 335–355, 1997.

[15] T. C. Schelling, "Dynamic models of segregation," The Journal of Mathematical Sociology, vol. 1, no. 2, pp. 143–186, 1971. https://doi.org/10.1080/0022250X.1971.9989794. Retrieved: Sept. 2024.

[16] U. Wilensky and K. Reisman, "Connected Science: Learning Biology through Constructing and Testing Computational Theories -- an Embodied Modeling Approach," International Journal of Complex Systems, vol. M. 234, pp. 1–12, 1998.

[17] U. Wilensky and K. Reisman, "Thinking like a Wolf, a Sheep, or a Firefly: Learning Biology through Constructing and Testing Computational Theories-An Embodied Modeling Approach," Cognition and Instruction, vol. 24, no. 2, pp. 171–209, 2006. http://www.jstor.org/stable/27739831. Retrieved: Sept. 2024.

[18] N. Vriend, "ACE Models of Endogenous Interactions," in Handbook of Computational Economics, vol. 2, 2006, pp. 1047-1079, doi: 10.1016/S1574-0021(05)02021-6. Retrieved: Sept. 2024.

[19] A. T. Young, "What does it take for a roving bandit to settle down? Theory and an illustrative history of the Visigoths," Public Choice, vol. 168, pp. 75–102, 2016. https://doi.org/10.1007/s11127-016-0350-7. Retrieved: Sept. 2024.

COSMOS Simulator: A Software Tool for Construction-Process Modelling and Simulation

Jirawat Damrianant
Department of Civil Engineering,
Faculty of Engineering, Thammasat School of Engineering,
Thammasat University,
Pathum Thani, Thailand
E-mail: djirawat@engr.tu.ac.th

Sakkaphant Meklersuewong
Department of Civil Engineering,
Faculty of Engineering, Thammasat School of Engineering,
Thammasat University,
Pathum Thani, Thailand
E-mail: sakkaphant@gmail.com

***Abstract*—Computer simulation software is an essential tool for efficiently simulating complex processes. Construction Oriented Simulation MOdelling System (COSMOS) Simulator is a program developed specifically for simulating models created using COSMOS methodology, a modified Petri Net designed for simulating construction-based operations. However, unlike some existing Petri Net-based simulators, which may require a deep understanding of Petri Net theory, COSMOS is designed to be intuitive and accessible to construction professionals. Although previous studies have used the COSMOS Simulator to simulate various construction processes and documented its accuracy, no published work directly describes the simulator itself. This article aims to provide a detailed description and illustration of the COSMOS Simulator's features, especially its ability to model and simulate specific construction behaviours. This paper offers a resource for researchers and practitioners interested in leveraging COSMOS for their construction modelling and simulation needs.**

Keywords-COSMOS; Simulator; Construction; Process; Petri Nets.

I. INTRODUCTION

Process modelling and simulation are valuable approaches for construction engineering. However, a suitable software tool is necessary to simulate complex construction operations. The need for construction simulation software has been driven by the increasing complexity of construction projects and the need for effective planning and resource management tools.

The development of simulation software or systems has been discussed in [1] and summarised as follows. Early systems like the Micro-Computerized CYCLic Operation Network (MicroCYCLONE) and the Dynamic Interface for Simulation of Construction Operations (DISCO) laid the groundwork for the field. Still, their adoption was often limited by the specialised knowledge required to use them. The emergence of object-oriented programming and discrete-event simulation paradigms led to the development of more user-friendly and versatile tools like the Construction Operation Simulation Tool (COST) and the Construction Object Oriented Process Simulation (COOPS) system. However, the inherent complexity of construction processes, with their inherent uncertainties and dynamic interactions, continued to pose challenges for simulation modelling.

As detailed in this paper, the COSMOS Simulator presents a significant advancement in construction process modelling and simulation. The software can simulate models created using the COSMOS methodology [2], a modified Petri Net designed to facilitate simulation modelling of construction-based operations. The methodology introduces new nodes, arcs, and attributes to capture complex construction behaviours, improving the ease and realism of modelling for simulation and analysis. The article [2] details how these extended elements interact to represent various construction scenarios, showcasing their flexibility in handling the complexities of construction. However, unlike some Petri Net-based simulators that may demand a deep understanding of Petri Net theory, COSMOS is crafted to be easily accessible for construction professionals.

This article addresses a gap in the existing literature by providing a direct and detailed description of the COSMOS Simulator's features and capabilities. While previous studies have utilised the simulator for various construction simulations (some in Thai) [3]-[11], and the software's accuracy has also been confirmed and reported in several articles (some in Thai) [5][7][8][10], a dedicated publication outlining its functionalities was lacking. This paper fills that void. The article offers a detailed description and illustration of the distinctive features of the COSMOS Simulator, notably its capability to model behaviours not typically accessible in other Petri Net simulators, such as [12]-[16]. These features include elements like Header, Follower, Buffer, Pipe, End Arc, and DPA, which can manage continuous processes and dynamically progressive activities commonly encountered in specific construction processes. The COSMOS Simulator's user interface and key components will be described in Section II. A discussion, conclusion, and suggestions for future work will be provided at the end of the article in Sections III and IV.

II. Descriptions of User Interface and Key Components

This section will review COSMOS's user interface and explain the essential components of the COSMOS Simulator. Figure 1 displays the homepage of the COSMOS Simulator's user interface, which can be accessed by selecting "Model" in the "view mode selector" panel. It should be noted that the Model mode is pre-selected by default. The system interface comprises several key components: the Menu Bar, Simulation-Run Controller Panel, Simulation Control Bar Properties Palette, Modelling Element Panel, Model Drawing Area, Status Bar, and View Mode Selector. The following subsections will comprehensively describe each of these significant components of the COSMOS Simulator.

A. Menu Bar

The menu bar in Figure 1 is divided into three tabs: Files, Settings, and Help. Each tab contains commands for manipulating files and software settings, such as creating a new file, opening an existing file, saving files, and changing font and grid settings.

B. Simulation-Run Controller Panel

To operate the simulation, users interact with the buttons on the "simulation-run controller panel". This panel contains several buttons as follows;

"Continuous Run" initiates a continuous simulation with animation as transitions fire and tokens move.

"Flash Run" simulates without displaying any animation, only providing the simulation's results unless the user specifies that animation should be shown.

"Pause" temporarily halts the simulation.

"Reset" brings the simulation back to its initial state.

"Previous Step" steps the simulation backwards by one step.

"Previous Event" steps the simulation backwards by one event.

"Next Event" steps the simulation forward by one event.

"Next Step" steps the simulation forward by one step.

See Figure 2 for the locations of these buttons in the user interface.

It is important to note that running the simulation by a step or by an event differs in terms of how the animation displays tokens residing in the places between adjacent transitions. When simulating by an event, the animation does not show tokens temporarily residing in the places, whereas simulating by a step does display these tokens.

C. Simulation Control Bar

Before running a simulation, users can define a seed number in the "Seed" field of the "simulation control bar" (see Figure 1). The specified seed number is the initiator for generating a random number stream using the Linear Congruential Method. This stream is subsequently utilised to generate random samplings, including the firing duration, referred to as 'Service Time' within the COSMOS Simulator. Service time is sometimes stochastic; in such cases, the generated random numbers are used to determine the service time of the transitions each time they fire. These stochastic durations are governed by Probability Density Functions (PDF) specified by the users (See Figure 3). Additionally, the COSMOS Simulator utilises the stream to determine events for transition firings, whether they will fire or not. The determination is based on the probability ratios associated with transitions set by the users. These transition probabilities can be employed to resolve conflicts among transitions, should they arise.

The control bar offers additional functionalities. The Time Interval field allows users to specify the display frequency of the simulation run. For example, suppose the COSMOS simulation begins at time = 0, and the Time Interval is set to 5 minutes. In that case, the Simulator will visualise the run at 5, 10, 15, 20 minutes, and so on, showcasing the transition's firing and token movement animations at those time intervals. The simulation's speed can be adjusted using the Play Speed slider. Additionally, the Time Limit field allows users to define a specific time at which the simulation will be forced to terminate, even if its natural stopping conditions are not met.

D. Modelling Element Panel

The COSMOS modelling elements are located in the "modelling element panel", as shown in Figure 1. The panel contains various buttons representing different modelling element types, except for the top-left button which serves as the selection mode. Clicking on any of these buttons allows users to enter the mode for placing the selected element type on the "model drawing area." The first four elements in the panel, located next to the selection mode, are the common Petri Nets elements: Token, Place, Transition, and Arc.

1) Place: A place element has two primary attributes: capacity and marking. Capacity refers to the maximum number of tokens that can be stored in a place at any given time, whereas marking indicates the current number of tokens present in the place. For instance, consider a Petri Net shown in Figure 1, where place P1 has a capacity of 4 tokens and currently contains one token. The current marking and capacity of the place are denoted by the numbers on the top-right corner as "1/4". A black area resembling a pie chart is used to visually represent the ratio between the marking and the capacity of the place.

2) Transition: Transitions in the COSMOS Simulator have several primary attributes that determine their behaviours during the simulation. These attributes include priority, probability, service time, and max firing queue. Figure 1 provides an example of a transition's properties palette (on the right-hand side of the figure), which displays its primary attributes. Priority and probability are used to resolve conflicts among transitions demanding tokens from the same place. Service time is the firing duration of the transition, which can be a constant value or a probability distribution. Users can change the firing duration type by clicking the "Edit" button in the properties palette. Figure 3 shows the properties editor for transition T1, which allows the user to specify the firing duration as a triangular distribution with minimum, mode, and maximum values of 5, 12, and 18 time units, respectively.

The term "max firing queue" refers to the maximum number of times a transition can fire simultaneously. This feature is handy for modelling certain construction behaviours. For example, when two loaders are working together to load three trucks, with each loader handling one truck at a time, there are instances when loading activities for two trucks occur simultaneously or overlap. The "max firing queue" feature can be used in this case.

Consider the initial state of a truck-loading model, as shown in Figure 4. Three trucks are located at P1, while two loaders are stationed at P2. By setting the maximum firing queue to 2, as shown in Figure 5, T1 can fire twice overlappingly. When firing, the number 2 displayed in the middle of T1 indicates that the transition handles two firings simultaneously. If the maximum firing queue were set to 1 (the default value), T1 could only fire once at a time. This scenario would not accurately reflect the real-world situation in which two loaders are available to handle the loading process simultaneously. Finally, the model in Figure 6 represents the circumstances when one truck is still being loaded while another truck has already finished loading. The number 1 displayed in the middle of T1 indicates that only one firing is being handled by T1 at this point in time.

3) Token and Arc: Tokens and arcs in the COSMOS Simulator serve the same function as those in common Petri Nets. In the current version of the simulator, all tokens and arcs are black and do not have any additional attributes or colours.

4) Condition Arc: Condition arcs in the COSMOS Simulator share similarities with inhibitor arcs found in modified Petri Nets, although substantial disparities exist between them. While the weight on a typical inhibitor arc is fixed at "equals zero," a condition arc possesses the flexibility to adopt any integer value as its weight, thereby enabling the expression of conditions in either equality or inequality formats. For instance, a condition arc's weight can be designated as "greater than or equal to 4." Additional instances illustrating the practical applications of condition arcs can be found in references [5][9] or a brief model delineated in Figure 7.

The model depicted in Figure 7 entails the transportation of 8 pieces of precast elements from a casting plant to a construction site. A loader situated at the plant facilitates the loading of precast elements onto a truck for transportation while also managing the unfinished precast elements within the plant. Nonetheless, the primary emphasis of this operation lies in the transportation of the eight precast elements. Consequently, the simulation of the process necessitates termination upon the completion of transporting the eight elements to the construction site and the subsequent return of the truck to the plant. In this model, a condition arc with a weight of ">= 1" (greater than or equal to one) is employed to govern the cessation of the process.

These features of condition arcs are handy for modellers who require control over specific logic or conditions in their construction process models. The features allow modellers to make their models more concise.

5) Header, Follower, Buffer, Pipe, and End Arc: Specific construction activities can only begin after their respective preceding activities have operated for a designated period. However, the completion of preceding activities is not mandatory before commencing the succeeding ones. When two or more activities share this interdependent relationship, they are classified as overlapping activities. To manage such overlapping activities, the COSMOS Simulator utilises five modelling elements: Header, Follower, Buffer, Pipe, and End Arc. Figure 8 displays the symbols of the five elements in the "modelling element panel" of the COSMOS Simulator.

A header is a unique transition type representing the first activity in a series of overlapping activities. Like a normal transition, it can be enabled and fired (shot). The primary function of a header is to convert discrete units of work into continuous units, represented as a percentage. When a header shoots, it sends portions of the work through pipes and a buffer to the next activity in the series. Additional details regarding the shooting mechanism and the functionality of headers can be found in [3].

A follower can be regarded as a particular type of transition, similar to a header. However, followers represent subsequent activities instead of representing the first activity in a series of overlapping activities. Like headers, followers release portions of continuous work through shootings. The quantity of work released from each shooting of a follower is equal to the shooting percentage specified in the header of the series. The shooting criteria for a follower are the same as those for a normal transition, with the additional condition that the released quantity of work from the preceding element (either a header or another follower) must be available in the input buffer of the follower. Further details on the functionality of followers can be found in [3].

A buffer is a special type of place where portions of the quantity of work released from headers or followers are stored. Buffers are connected to headers or followers via pipes. It's important to note that tokens cannot reside in buffers, and buffers have an unlimited capacity.

A pipe is a particular type of arc used to represent the flow of work released from headers or followers. In other words, pipes are used to send portions of work resulting from shootings of headers or followers. Pipes can only connect headers or followers to buffers and buffers to followers.

The COSMOS Simulator utilises an "end arc" to conclude overlapping series when the shooting percentage of the final follower reaches 100%. Once this threshold is met, the end arc sends a token or tokens to the connected outgoing place, with the number of tokens depending on the weight of the arc. This mechanism effectively terminates the series and ensures proper execution of the simulation.

Sakkaphant Meklersuewong and Jirawat Damrianant [10] demonstrate the use of the five elements (header, follower, buffer, pipe, and end arc) in a sample application to simulate overlapping activities in a concreting and waste-handling operation.

6) Dynamically Progressive Activity (DPA): Dynamically Progressive Activity (DPA) is defined in COSMOS as an activity whose duration varies due to the increase in the amount of work for each iteration. DPAs commonly occur in linear construction processes such as road construction and drainage pipe installation. For example, in reinforced-concrete road construction, the "moving to placing spot" activity will have a longer duration as the length of the road being constructed increases with each iteration of the placement. This is because the starting point of the placement area remains stationary while the placing spots get further away for each round of the placement. As a result, the distances between the beginning of the placement zone and the placing spots increase, thereby increasing the duration of the "moving to placing spot" activity performed by ready-mixed concrete trucks.

If a DPA's working rate and amount of work are known, its activity duration can be calculated. For instance, in reinforced-concrete road construction, suppose a concrete truck moves between the starting point of the placement area and a placing spot at an average speed of 10 km/hr or 166.67 m/min (this represents the working rate), and the distance between the beginning of the placement zone and the placing spot is 100 m (this represents the amount of work). In this case, the duration required for the truck in the "moving to placing spot" activity will be 0.6 minutes, indicating that, on average, the truck can cover a distance of 100 m within 0.6 minutes. Therefore, for distances of 200 m, 300 m, and 400 m, the truck will require 1.2, 1.8, and 2.4 minutes, respectively, to complete the activity.

After determining the duration of a DPA, users can input this information into the corresponding activity within the COSMOS Simulator. Subsequently, the simulator will calculate the duration of each iteration of the DPA by incrementally advancing the amount of work completed and using these values to simulate the process.

Figure 9 presents a concrete-road placement model, representing an operation similar to the abovementioned process. The model showcases the implementation of the DPA concept. Notably, a DPA element in the COSMOS Simulator is a unique type of transition that features a dynamically progressive firing duration. In the figure, the elements labelled "DPA1-Truck proceeds from the starting point of the placement area to the placing spot" and "DPA2-Truck returns to the starting location of the placement area" represent DPAs. When DPA1 fires for the first time, its firing duration will be zero since a truck can discharge concrete immediately upon reaching the starting point of the placement area without needing to move further forward. In the subsequent three iterations, the firing durations will be 0.6 minutes, 1.2 minutes, and 1.8 minutes as the placing points for the truck will be located 100 meters, 200 meters, and 300 meters away, respectively, from the beginning of the placement zone.

III. Discussion

Unlike some existing simulators, which may require a deep understanding of Petri Net theory, the COSMOS Simulator is designed to be intuitive and accessible to construction professionals. By incorporating unique modelling elements, COSMOS allows the representation of complex construction behaviours often overlooked in traditional Petri Net simulators. The ability to model overlapping activities, dynamically progressive activities, and resource constraints set the COSMOS Simulator apart, providing a more accurate and realistic simulation environment tailored to the construction industry's specific needs.

Compared to the existing solutions, primarily represented by general-purpose Petri Net simulators, COSMOS demonstrates several advantages. Including construction-specific modelling elements allows the representation of unique construction behaviours. The focus on practical applicability makes COSMOS more accessible to construction professionals compared to simulators with limited construction-specific features. Furthermore, COSMOS's ability to model complex resource management scenarios and dynamic changes in activity durations provides a more comprehensive simulation environment for construction projects.

While COSMOS represents a significant step forward, it is essential to acknowledge its limitations and potential areas for future development. The simulator's primary focus on discrete-event simulation may limit its applicability to continuous processes or systems with complex interactions. Additionally, although COSMOS can simulate dynamic processes, its current version may have limitations in incorporating real-time data from construction sites, which is crucial for achieving a true digital representation of construction processes. Future research and development efforts can focus on expanding COSMOS's capabilities in these areas, further enhancing its value and impact in the construction industry. The current version of the COSMOS Simulator is available online [17].

IV. Conclusion and Future Work

This paper provided a comprehensive description and illustration of the distinctive features of the COSMOS Simulator, a computer program designed to simulate construction processes effectively. COSMOS accounts for real-world construction behaviours such as:

- Concurrent execution of similar activities through "max firing queue" settings.

- Overlapping or interleaved activities facilitated by headers, followers, buffers, pipes, and end arcs.
- Simulation of Dynamically Progressive Activities (DPAs), where duration varies based on workload, commonly seen in tasks like asphalt paving.

Notably, these modelling elements and features—headers, followers, buffers, pipes, end arcs, and DPAs—are unique to COSMOS, enabling the simulation of specific behaviours found in construction, and they are not available in other simulation tools.

Apart from normal arcs, COSMOS also has condition arcs similar to inhibitor arcs in modified Petri Nets but allow more flexibility. They can have any integer weight, enabling the expression of equality or inequality conditions.

COSMOS has been successfully used to model and simulate various aspects of construction. However, further research is needed to explore the needs and gather feedback from diverse users. This information will be crucial in enhancing the COSMOS system to make it even more effective in simulating construction processes.

This paper offered a resource for researchers and practitioners interested in leveraging COSMOS for their construction modelling and simulation needs.

Despite its emphasis on functionality for construction practitioners, the COSMOS Simulator and its associated methodology can be used to model and simulate any discrete event process.

Future research and development efforts will focus on expanding COSMOS's capabilities to incorporate real-time data from construction sites. Additionally, it would be beneficial to extend COSMOS's capabilities to simulate construction processes with even more complex interactions. The simulation of more complex interactions could be achieved by adding appropriate control statements, enabling users to have finer control over the behaviours of the COSMOS models and aligning them more closely with the actual behaviours of construction work in the fields.

REFERENCES

[1] B. Visartsakul and J. Damrianant, "A review of BIM and simulation as virtual representations under the Digital Twin concept," Eng. J., vol. 27(1), pp. 11-27, Jan. 2023, doi:10.4186/ej.2023.27.1.11.

[2] J. Damrianant, "COSMOS: A Discrete-Event Modeling Methodology for Construction Processes," Int. J. Internet Enterp. Manag., vol. 1, pp. 128-152, Apr. 2003, doi:10.1504/IJIEM.2003.003209.

[3] J. Damrianant and R. R. Wakefield, "A Petri Net-Based Methodology for Modelling of Overlapping Activity Processes," The Second International Conference on Construction Process Re-engineering. CPR-99, Sydney, 1999, pp. 375-386.

[4] S. Meklersuewong and J. Damrianant, "Energy Reduction in Road Construction," The Third International Symposium on Engineering, Energy and Environments (ISEEE-3), Bangkok, 2013, pp. 523-532.

[5] J. Damrianant, "Optimization of Supply Trains in Tunnel Boring Operation Using Tunnel Boring Machines," The Sixth International Conference on Advances in Civil, Structural and Mechanical Engineering (CSM-18) Zurich, 2018, pp. 8-12. doi:10.15224/978-1-63248-150-4-23.

[6] J. Damrianant and T. Panrangsri, "Resource Management Using COSMOS Modeling and Simulation System to Lessen Concrete-Placing Duration," (in Thai) Thai J. Sci. Tech., vol. 7(5), pp. 553-566, Aug. 2018, doi:10.14456/tjst.2018.50.

[7] N. Suri and J. Damrianant, "Comparing Construction Process Simulation between the Arena and Cosmos Programs," (in Thai). Eng. J. Research Development, vol. 30(4), pp. 89-104, Oct. 2019, ISSN: 2730-2733.

[8] B. Visartsakul and J. Damrianant, "Determining Costs and Time Required for Building Construction by Using 3D Structural Models, Unit Costs, Productivity Rates, and Project Simulations," (in Thai) Eng. J. Research Development, vol. 31(4), pp. 63-76, Oct. 2020, ISSN: 2730-2733.

[9] J. Damrianant, "Track Management Approaches for Underground Tunnel Construction," Thai J. Sci. Tech., vol. 10(5), pp. 621-634, Sep. 2021, ISSN: 2286-7333.

[10] S. Meklersuewong and J. Damrianant, "Evaluating the COSMOS Software Ecosystem for Domain-Specific Construction Process Simulation," Int. Rev. Model. Simul., vol.15(3), pp. 179-188, Jun. 2022, doi:10.15866/iremos.v15i3.20268.

[11] J. Damrianant, "Comparison of Process and Project Duration Assessment Approaches for an Industrial Water-System Installation Project Using Estimation Method and COSMOS Program," (in Thai) J. KMUTNB, vol. 33(1), pp. 127-139. Jan. 2023, doi:10.14416/j.kmutnb.2022.06.004.

[12] M. A. Drighiciu and D. C. Cismaru, "Modeling a Water Bottling Line Using Petri Nets," Annals of the University of Craiova. Electr. Eng. Ser., vol. 37, pp. 110–115, 2013, ISSN: 1842-4805.

[13] M. Herajy, F. Liu, C. Rohr, and M. Heiner, "Snoopy's Hybrid Simulator: A Tool to Construct and Simulate Hybrid Biological Models," BMC Systems Biology, vol. 11(71), pp. 1-16, Jul. 2017, doi:10.1186/s12918-017-0449-6

[14] R. Davidrajuh, D. Krenczyk, and B. Skolud, "Finding Clusters in Petri Nets. An Approach Based on GPenSIM," Model. Identif. Control, vol 40(1), pp. 1-10, Jan. 2019, doi:10.4173/mic.2019.1.1.

[15] E. Kučera, et al., "New Software Tool for Modeling and Control of Discrete-Event and Hybrid Systems Using Timed Interpreted Petri Nets," Applied Sciences, vol. 10(15), pp. 5027, Jul. 2020, doi:10.3390/app10155027.

[16] V. B. Kumbharl and M. S. Chavan, "A Review of Petri Net Tools and Recommendations," Proceedings of the International Conference on Applications of Machine Intelligence and Data Analytics (ICAMIDA 2022), ICAMIDA 2022, ACSR 105, May 2023, pp. 710–721, doi:10.2991/978-94-6463-136-4_61.

[17] COSMOS Simulator. [Online]. Available from: https://drive.google.com/file/d/1qpxEvIq9TDNfynrqt_Wj5VEHGE3uBW53/view?usp=drive_link.

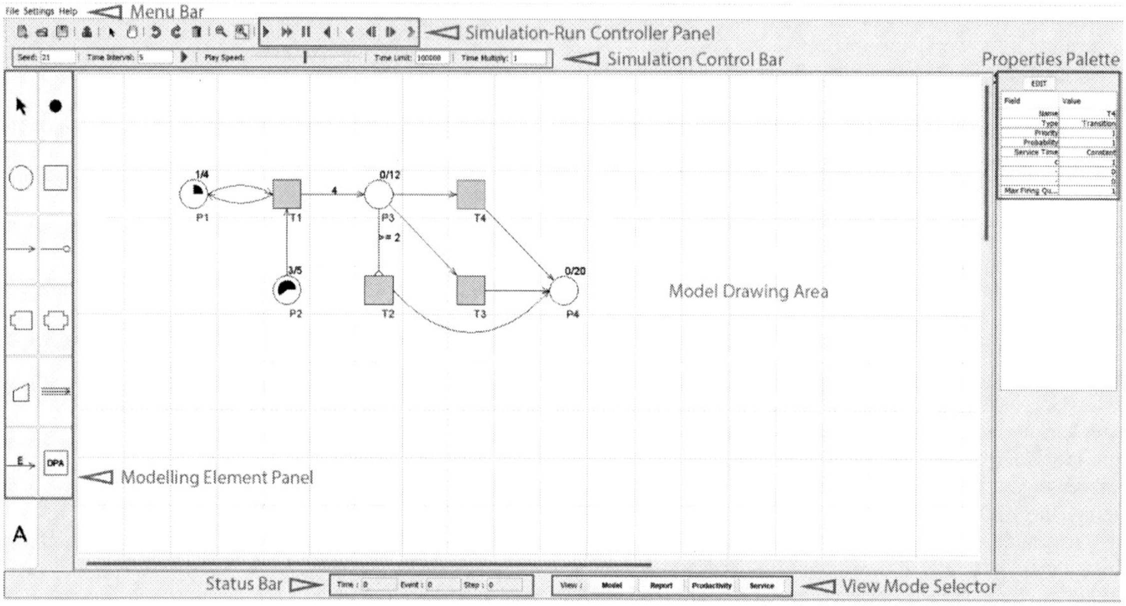

Figure 1. Homepage of COSMOS Simulator's user interface.

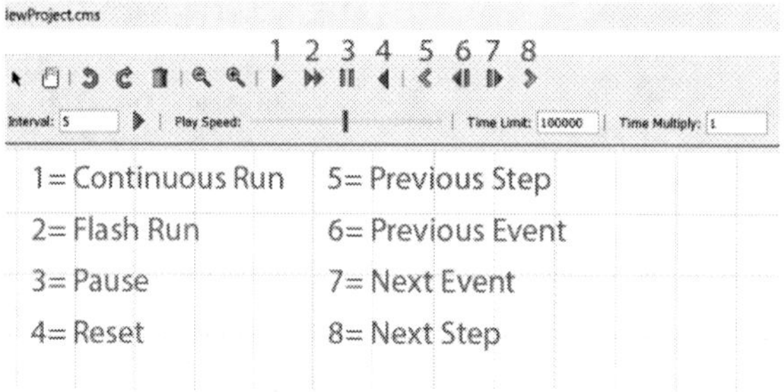

Figure 2. Simulation-Run Controller Panel.

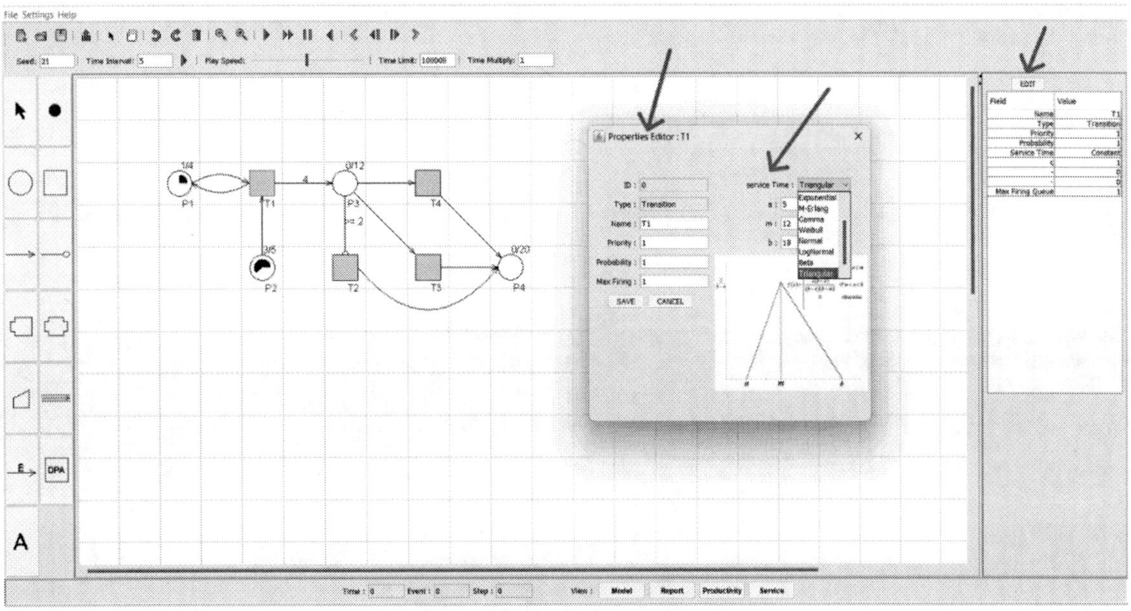

Figure 3. Properties Editor of Transition.

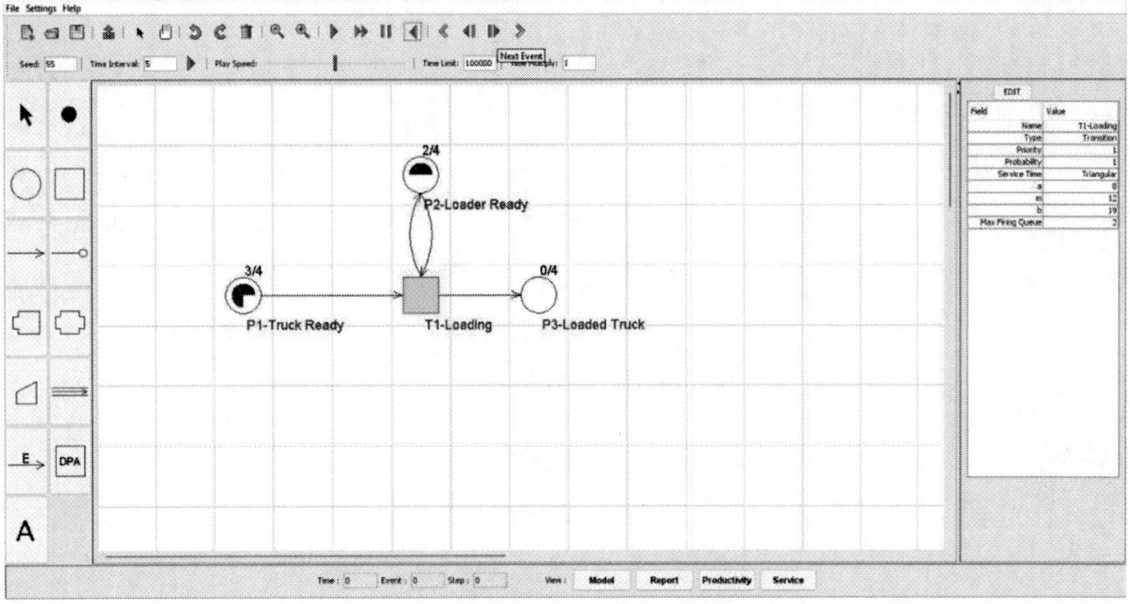

Figure 4. Model illustrating “Max Firing Queue” Feature (State 1).

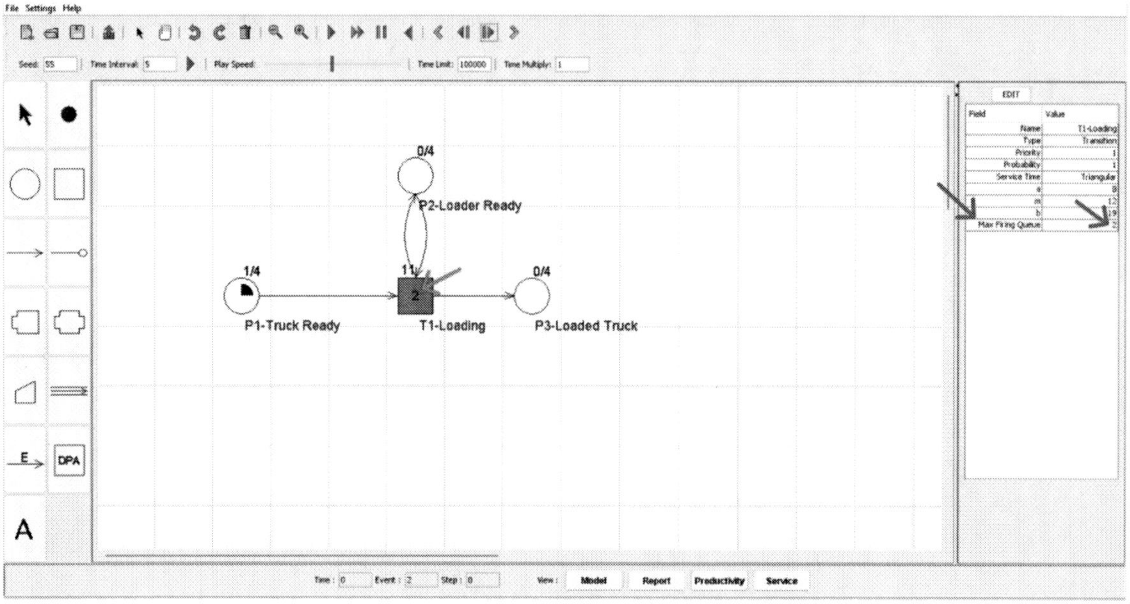

Figure 5. Model illustrating "Max Firing Queue" Feature (State 2).

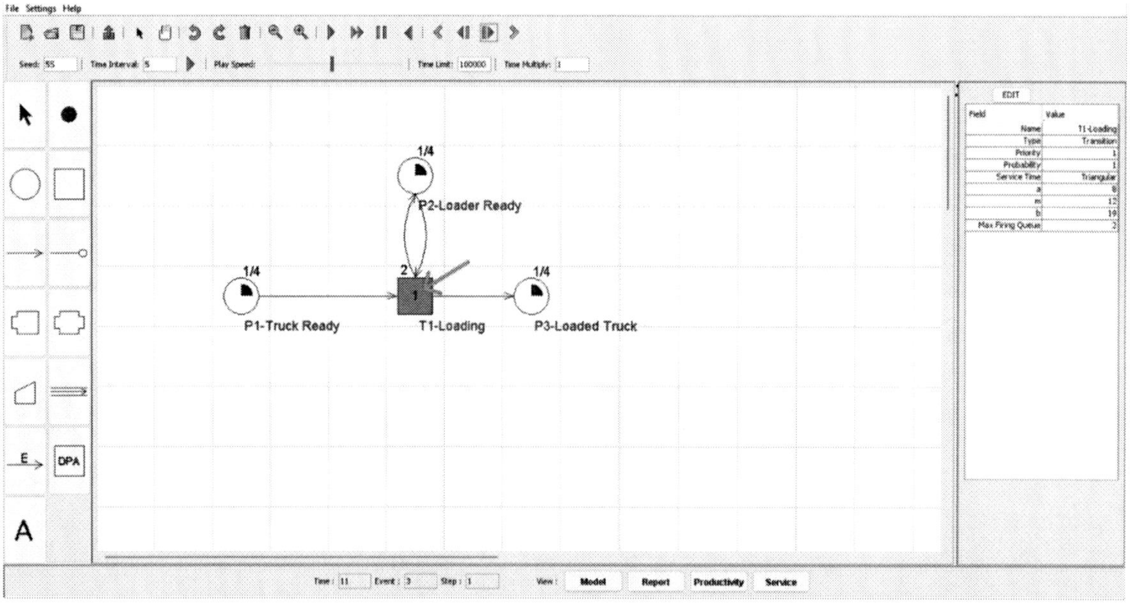

Figure 6. Model illustrating "Max Firing Queue" Feature (State 3).

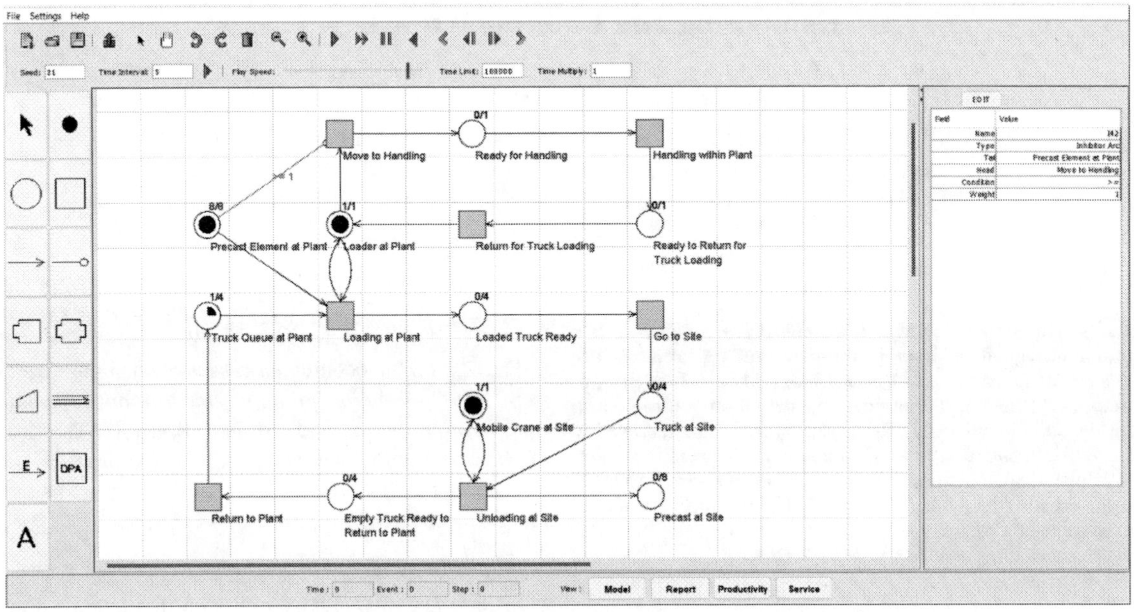

Figure 7. Model illustrating sample application of "Condition Arc".

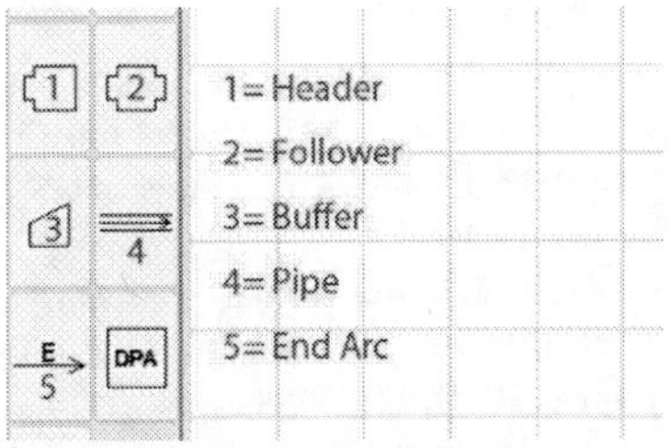

Figure 8. Header, Follower, Buffer, Pipe, and End Arc in Modelling Element Panel of COSMOS Simulator.

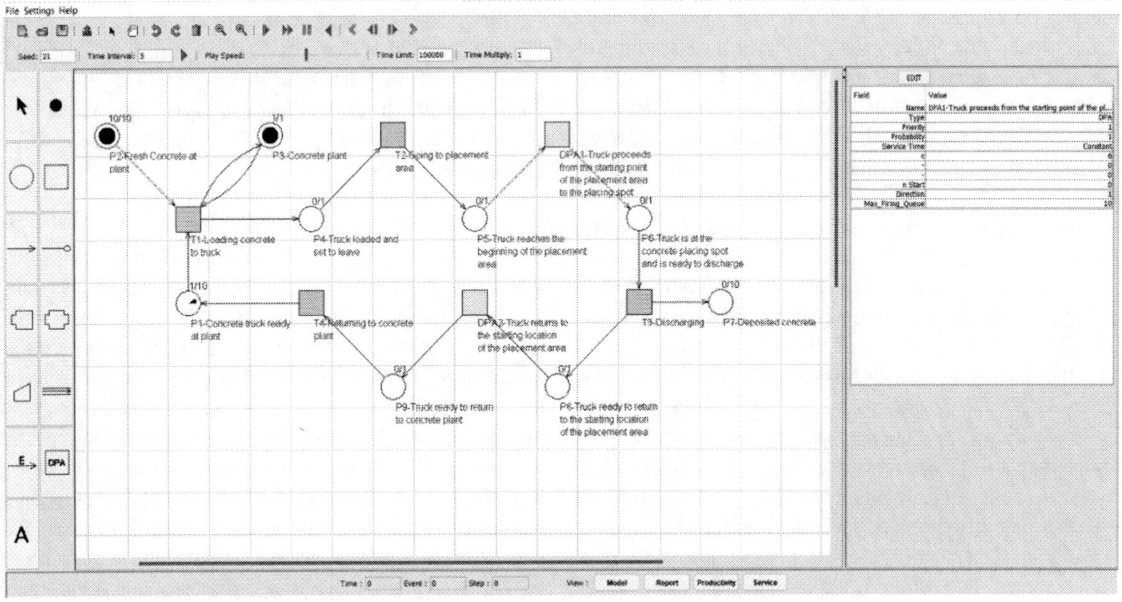

Figure 9. Dynamically Progressive Activities (DPAs) in a Concrete-Road Placement Model.

Reusable Building Blocks for Agent-Based Simulations: Towards a Method for Composing and Building ABM/LUCC

Eric Innocenti *, Dominique Prunetti *, Marielle Delhom †, Corinne Idda *
*UMR CNRS 6240, LISA Research Laboratory, University of Corsica Pasquale Paoli, Corte, France
e-mail:{eric.innocenti | prunetti_d, | idda_c}@univ-corse.fr
†UMR CNRS 6134, SPE Research Laboratory, University of Corsica Pasquale Paoli, Corte, France
e-mail: marielle.delhom@univ-corse.fr

***Abstract*—The *5-Steps Simplified Modelling Process* (*5-SSIMP*) is a method designed to develop modular and reusable *Agent-Based Models of Land Use and Cover Change* (*ABM/LUCC*) in an interdisciplinary context. It is based on the definition of three types of *Reusable Building Blocks* (*RBBs*): *Conceptual-RBB* (*conRBB*), *Computer-RBB* (*comRBB*), and *Executable-RBB* (*exeRBB*). We present a practical modelling example based on the *5-SSIMP* method for creating an *ABM/LUCC* applied to the socio-economic tourism system of Corsica.**

Keywords-Modelling method; ABM/LUCC; RBB.

I. Introduction

The computer simulation of "*Agent-Based Models of Land Use and Cover Change*" (*ABM/LUCC*) represents an inherently interdisciplinary research field, integrating computer science, software engineering, economics, geography, social sciences. Within this context, the intrinsic complexity of the spatial socio-economic systems under study necessitates a rigorous method to ensure the coherence, reliability, and validity of the simulation models. This is particularly pertinent to the specialisation of *Agent-Based Models* (*ABM*). The *5-Steps Simplified Modelling Process* (*5-SSIMP*) presented in this paper, is a stringent modelling and simulation method dedicated to the development of modular and reusable *ABM/LUCC* and their simulation experiments. Additionally, *5-SSIMP* enhances collaboration among the various disciplines involved. The process begins with a *conceptual model* that specifies the key elements of the system and progresses to the *computer modules* of the *executable model* in the digital world. During the *5-SSIMP* modelling process, modellers isolate and characterise these key elements in intermediate abstract and concrete models, grouping both generic and context-specific characteristics. The generic characteristics correspond to *Reusable Building Blocks* (*RBB*) and they group similar functionalities. The *5-SSIMP* process necessitates the definition of three types of *RBB*: *conceptual-RBB* (*conRBB*), *computer-RBB* (*comRBB*), and *executable-RBB* (*exeRBB*). In this paper, we explain how to characterise these elements in *ABM/LUCC* through the *5-SSIMP* process, which we review in Section 2. In section 3, we introduce the concept of *RBB*, key elements of this process, ensuring the modularity and reusability of the concepts, components, and codes involved. In section 4, an implementation example focused on the creation of an *ABM/LUCC* of the Corsican socio-economic tourism system is presented. In Section 5, we conclude and present the future perspectives of this research in computer simulation.

II. 5-SSIMP Method

The *5-SSIMP* modelling process is divided into five essential steps: (1) *Conceptualisation*, (2) *Integration*, (3) *Implementation*, (4) *Simulation*, and (5) *Data Analysis*. The production of *RBB* pertains to steps (1) to (3) of the process, which we refer to as the "*modelling phase*". The (4) to (5) steps of the process, refer to as the "*simulation phase*".

A. Modelling phase

In the *(1)-Conceptualisation* step, modellers simplify the real system by formulating a conceptual model, identifying key components and their relationships. During the *(2)-Integration* step, modellers translate the conceptual model into a computer model by defining appropriate objects, modules, and links. In the *(3)-Implementation* step, modellers convert the computer model into an executable model. They use computer programming languages and techniques for this, including *Object-Oriented Programming* (*OOP*) and *Design Patterns* (*DP*) [1]. As illustrated in Figure 1, the executable model is continuously improved through the iterative cycle of continuous adjustments (iterations).

B. Simulation phase

During the *(4)-Simulation* step, modellers validate and verify the model with rigorous tests to ensure the accuracy and reliability of the *simulated data*, comparing it with *real data* when possible. In the *(5)-Data Analysis* step, modellers finalise the *executable model* for routine practical use, ensuring it is reliable, robust, and efficient.

III. Reusable Building Block Concept

We have seen that the *5-SSIMP* modelling process is divided into five distinct stages, providing a clear and methodical structure for constructing an *ABM/LUCC* in an interdisciplinary context. During the first three stages, modellers identify and isolate key elements characterising the complex system, defining intermediate *abstract* and *concrete models*. These elements possess characteristics that are both generic and specific to the study context. Elements with generic characteristics are grouped into *RBBs* within the intermediate models, organising reusable structures and functionalities in a modular manner. Each *RBB* encapsulates a generic aspect of the intermediate model, such as generic agent behaviours, generic social interactions, or generic economic dynamics.

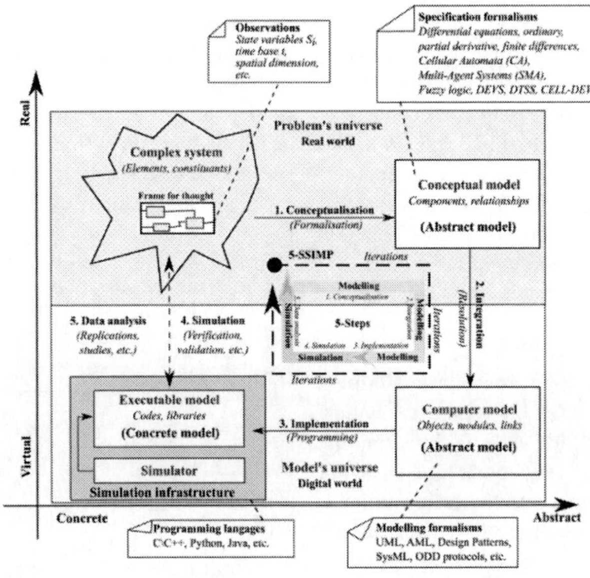

Figure 1. The *5-SSIMP* process is an iterative method for creating modular and reusable *ABM*, facilitating interdisciplinarity.

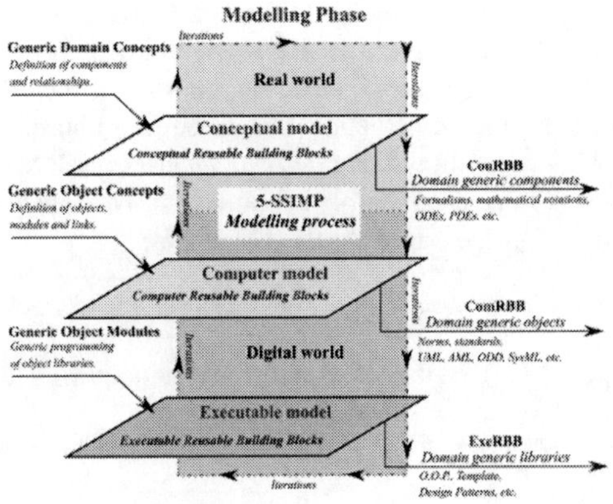

Figure 2. The central concept of *Reusable Building Block* (*RBB*), in accordance with the *5-SSIMP* modelling process.

As illustrated in Figure 2, this organisation of models into blocks promotes: (1) - the updating or replacement of blocks, maintenance, and evolution of the executable model during iterations (*modularity*); (2) - the creation of code libraries, enabling the sharing and reuse of proven code in other simulation projects (*reusability*). (3) - researchers in economics, sociology, and computer science can collaborate more easily by using and adapting these generic modules according to their specific needs.

A. Definition of conRBB

A *Conceptual Reusable Building Block* (*conRBB*) is a type of *RBB* produced in stage (1) of the conceptualisation process in *5-SSIMP*. *conRBBs* are developed using specification formalisms (rules, notations, formal languages, etc.), such as mathematical notations, *Ordinary Differential Equations* (*ODEs*), *specification of Discrete EVent System* (*DEVS* [2]), etc. *conRBBs* characterise in conceptual models the key generic components and their relationships as *Generic Domain Concepts*, in a structured and reusable manner.

TABLE I. LINKS BETWEEN MODELS AND PRODUCTION TOOLS OF *Reusable Building Blocks* IN THE *5-SSIMP* PROCESS.

5-SSIMP Model	RBB	Modelling tools
Conceptual	*conRBB*	Formalisms, mathematical notations, ODEs, PDEs, etc.
Computer	*comRBB*	Norms, standards UML, AML, ODD, SysML, etc.
Executable	*exeRBB*	P.O.O., Templates, Design Patterns, etc.

B. Definition of comRBB

A *Computer Reusable Building Block* (*comRBB*) is another type of *RBB*. It is produced in stage (2) of the integration process in *5-SSIMP*. *comRBBs* ensure coherence, standardisation, and reusability of generic objects across various simulation projects. They consist of sets of generic objects usable in diverse fields of study as *Generic Object Concepts*. To achieve this, *comRBBs* are established according to computer standards and norms such as the *Unified Modelling Language* (*UML*) [3], *Agent Modelling Language* (*AML*) [4], *Overview, Design concepts, and Details* (*ODD*) [5], or the *Systems Modeling Language* (*SysML*) [6], etc. Numerous recent studies demonstrate that *DPs* significantly enhance the modularity and reusability of models in computer simulation [7]–[9].

C. Definition of exeRBB

An *Executable Reusable Building Block* (*exeRBB*) is a type of *RBB* produced in stage (3) of the implementation process in the *5-SSIMP* modelling process. These building blocks correspond to the generic code components of the *executable model* grouped as *Generic Object Modules*. They implement principles from *OOP* and *Generic Programming*, as conceived in the computer model, using *Templates* [10] and *DPs* [1]. *exeRBBs* contribute to the practical execution of computer simulations, providing *reusable blocks of code* and *pseudo-code* adaptable to various simulation projects. These are typically generic software libraries, offering significant advantages in achieving software productivity and reliability.

IV. Practical Example

An *Agent-Based Model of Land Use and Cover Change* (*ABM/LUCC*) is an *ABM* that integrates the spatial dynamics of a socio-economic system [11][12]. It is used in this example to simulate the virtual territory of economic agents who evolve according to rules of economic development and land competition. Decision-making processes are based on spatial socio-environmental factors, as well as the heterogeneity and imbalances observed in the real socio-economic system.

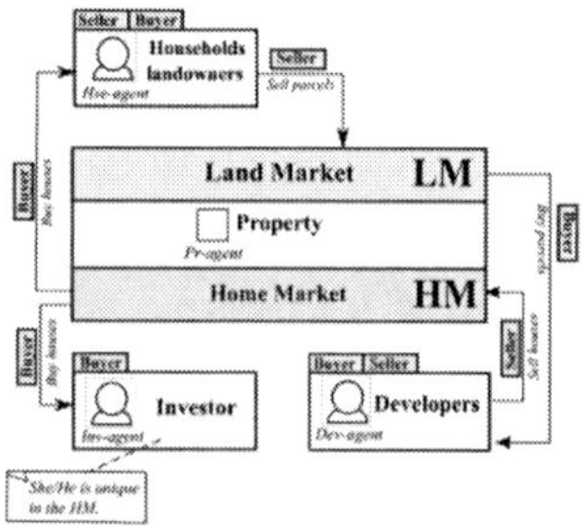

Figure 3. Organisation of agents and markets in the *conceptual model* [13].

The case study presented in this paper focuses on an *ABM/LUCC* that we employed to analyse the tourist areas in Corsica, which have experienced intense residential development in recent years. Its *conceptual model* is detailed in the article [13]. The complex system studied is a spatially defined territory, bordered by the sea and subject to socio-economic dynamics influenced by two main processes: a *Land Market - LM* and a *Home Market - HM*. In the *LM*, interactions occur between "*household seller agents owning land*" (agent-*Hse*) and "*developer buyer agents*" (agent-*Dev*). The *HM*, on the other hand, involves coordination between "*household buyer agents*" (agent-*Hse*) and a single "*investor buyer agent*" (agent-*Inv*). The agents-*Hse* and *Inv* compete in the *HM* to purchase houses built by the agents-*Dev*, who act as sellers in this *HM*. Figure 3 illustrates these organisation. The conceptual specification *MR POTATOHEAD* (*MPH - Model Representing Potential Objects Appearing in the Ontology of Humano-Environmental Actions and Decisions.*) is used in this case study to describe the complex socio-economic system of Corsica with two markets [14], [15, p.407]. It is a *Conceptual Design Pattern* (*CDP*) intended for the generic definition and organisation of key components and their relationships in the conceptual model of an *ABM/LUCC* [16]. The conceptual specification *MPH* allows for the standardised definition of *ABM/LUCC* with price formation processes between buyers and sellers and their decision-making processes, which combine deductive optimisation and inductive models of price expectation formation in generic agents. We use it here in its "*Property Market Edition* [17]" version to precisely characterise the *conRBB*. (For a more detailed article on the subject, interested readers can consult the following paper: [18].)

LM Market: Some *agent-Hse* own plots of land that are sold on the *LM* market. The decision-making process of an *agent-Hse* offering land for sale is based on the *conRBB Willingness to Accept* (*WTA*). In this example, the *WTA* considers the average (historical) selling prices $P_{t-1}(z_i)$ of similar plots with the same characteristics z_i according to 1.

$$WTA_{La}(z_i) = P_{t-1}(z_i) \tag{1}$$

In this same market, the decision-making process of an *agent-Dev* is based on the *conRBB Willingness to Pay* (*WTP*) for a given plot of land i. The *agent-Dev* make predictions about the price at which they can sell the house built on this plot and aim to achieve a profit margin rate on the total cost of the house.

$$WTP_m(z_i) = \frac{P_{H,i,t-1}(z_i, LivA_m) - C_{LivA}(z_i)\, LivA_m}{1+\pi_m} \tag{2}$$

where, $P_{H,i,t-1}(z_i, LivA_m)$ is the (past) average price paid for an equivalent house; $LivA_m$ is the living area of a house of a m type; π_m is the expected margin rate of the developer; $C_{LivA}(z_i)$ is the construction cost to build a house.

HM Market: In the *HM market*, *agent-Dev* sell the houses, i.e., *agent-Pr* fixed on the plan (properties), previously defined in the *LM market*, based on the *WTA* of 3.

$$WTA_{i,m}(z_i, LivA_m) = (1+\pi_m)\left(\overline{P_i}(z_i) + C_{LivA} LivA_m\right) \tag{3}$$

where $\overline{P_i}(z_i)$ is the cost incurred for acquiring the land parcel i.

In this housing market, the *WTP* (*conRBB*) of the sole *agent-Inv* is given by 4.

$$WTP_I(\eta) = \frac{1-(1+r)^{-T}}{r(1-\rho)(1+r)^{-T} + rT - 1 + (1+r)^{-T}} \gamma\zeta\varphi(\eta) \tag{4}$$

where $r \in [0,1]$ is the financial market interest rate, $\gamma \in [0,1]$ represents the net rental return coefficient (net of maintenance costs), ζ is the duration of the tourist season in days, $\varphi(\eta)$ is the average daily revenue for a tourist residence with corresponding characteristics, T denotes the average loan duration, $\rho(1+r)^{-T} P_I(\eta)$ is the house's residual value after T years, with $\rho \in [0,1]$.

Finally, in this market, the *WTP* (*conRBB*) of the *agent-Hse* is given by 5.

$$WTP_c(\eta) = \frac{(1+\delta_c)\left[(1+\delta_c)^T - 1\right]}{\delta_c} \frac{YD_c\left(V_c^{Max}\right)^2}{b^2 + \left(V_c^{Max}\right)^2} \tag{5}$$

where δ_c is the discount rate of the *agent-Hse*, V_c^{Max} is the maximal utility value the *agent-Hse* can obtained buying the house corresponding to this maximal value, YD_c is the amount of money that the *agent-Hse* spends on housing each period and b is the slope of the bid function. (For a more detailed presentation of the *conRBB* in this conceptual model, interested readers can refer to the articles [13], [18].) To quickly and easily obtain a functional *ABM/LUCC* prototype with these characteristics, featuring immediately usable objects and modules, we chose to integrate the conceptual model using the *NetLogo Design Pattern* (*NetLogo-DP*) proposed by *Seth Tisue* and *Uri Wilensky* [19].

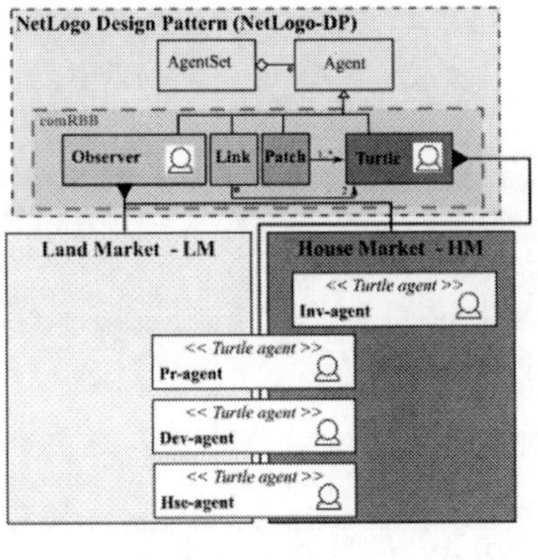

Figure 4. The *NetLogo-DP* allows for the simple construction of an *ABM/LUCC* with just four types of *comRBB*: an *omniscient observer* (*Observer*), *cells* (*Patches*), *turtles* (*Turtles*), and *links* (*Links*).

The *NetLogo-DP* is characterised by the generic agents of an *ABM* that can be easily implemented in the generic part of the executable model within the *NetLogo* simulation environment. In the presented case study, the agents of the *ABM/LUCC* are derived through increasing specialisation from four *comRBB* (highlighted in red in Figure 4) of the *NetLogo-DP*: an *omniscient observer* (*Observer*), *cells* (*Patches*), *turtles* (*Turtles*), and *links* (*Links*). The *comRBB* "*Observer*" should be considered as a unique agent responsible for monitoring the environment and issuing commands to the various other agents (mobile or fixed) present in the *ABM/LUCC* space. The *comRBB* "*Patches*" are space agents that represent fixed locations (cells). Thus, the *NetLogo-DP* offers a simple and effective means to construct an *ABM/LUCC* prototype (computer model) from just four *comRBB*. The implementation phase is the final step of modelling (Recall that the remaining steps (4) and (5) respectively deal with *simulation* and *data analysis* as illustrated in Figure 1.) the complex system in the *5-SSIMP* modelling process. In our case study, this step involves producing the code for the executable model using the *NetLogo* programming language. This requires us to adhere to the numerical schema of objects, modules, and links defined in the previous *computer model* (cf. Figure 4). The agents of the executable model are thus implemented in accordance with the *exeRBB breed* specific to the *NetLogo* programming environment.

Figure 5 is a code snippet showing how to use the generic syntax `breed[householdsAgt householdAgt]` of the *exeRBB* `breed` to define the *agent-Hse* of the *ABM/LUCC*. In this snippet, each *agent-Hse* has its own attributes specified using the `-own` command of the *exeRBB* `breed`. In

```
;HouSEhold Agents (HSE)
breed[householdsAgt householdAgt]
householdsAgt-own[
  HI_isHouseOwner?; Property owner
  H_isLandowner?; Landowner
  H_houseHoldCat; Socio-pro category
  H_disposable-budget; Budget prop. purchase
  HDI_leeway; Leeway
  H_discountRate; Discount rate
  H_maxValueHouseUtility; Maxi. utility value
  H_houseRef; Pro. rel. - Maxi. utility
  H_wealth; Non-wage income
  H_quarterlyInterestRate; Q.Int.rate]
```

Figure 5. Implementation of the *-Hse* agents in the computer model using the `breed` *exeRBB* from *NetLogo*.

NetLogo, using the `breed` directive allows for the simple and efficient prototyping of all agents in the *ABM/LUCC* within an executable model, thereby facilitating the exploration of behaviours and socio-economic properties within the complex system under study.

We simulate five policy scenarios designed to address Corsica's unique challenges and opportunities as a tourist destination, focusing on sustainable urban development and environmental sustainability:

1) Business As Usual (BAU): This baseline scenario extrapolates the continuation of current trends, providing a comparative benchmark to evaluate the effects of more interventionist policies.

2) Total Ban on Tourist Rental Investments (BTRI): Reflecting drastic yet plausible policy measures to curb the overdevelopment of tourist accommodations, this scenario evaluates the impact of entirely prohibiting new tourist rental investments.

3) Tax on Tourist Rental Investment Incomes (TTRI): This scenario introduces a tax, ranging from 0.01 to 0.5, on incomes derived from tourist rental investments. The rationale behind this measure is to deter excessive investment in tourist rentals by reducing their profitability, thereby influencing land market dynamics.

4) Coastal Zoning (CZ): This scenario mandates a minimum required distance from the coastline, ranging from 1 to 50 units, for any new tourist rental investments. Its objective is to preserve coastal regions and reduce the concentration of developments near the sea, which are often high-demand areas. Furthermore, considering the ecological sensitivity of Corsica's coastline, this policy imposes restrictions on new tourist rental investments near coastal areas to protect these vital habitats and maintain their accessibility for future generations.

5) CBD Zoning (CBD-Z): Similar to the coastal distance policy, this scenario mandates a minimum distance ranging from 1 to 50 units from the *CBD* for new tourist rental investments. The objective of this policy is to distribute tourist accommodations more evenly across the territory, thereby alleviating pressure on urban centres and promoting the development of underutilised areas. The Table II lists the

TABLE II. FIXED PARAMETERS

Input	Value
Percentage of low revenue households	54%
Percentage of middle revenue households	20%
Percentage of high revenue households	26%
Percentage of households that own their home	52%
Percentage of households that own a buildable parcel of land	87%
Share of households income spent on housing	0.3
Time Horizon (year)	20
Transport cost (€/km)	0.5404
Number of buildable parcels of land	2,500
Number of resident households	5,625
Number of developers	4
Number of Rent days	220
Slope of the bid function	0.8

fixed parameters used in the experiments. These values remain constant throughout the simulations to serve as a benchmark.

TABLE III. RANDOM UNIFORM VALUE PARAMETERS

Input	Value
Land Area (m^2)	$[500, 2500[$
Sea view Index	$[0.75, 23.25[$
Disposable budget of low revenue households	$[6200, 23200[$
Disposable budget of middle revenue households	$[10000, 40000[$
Disposable budget of high revenue households	$[11500, 71500[$
Disposable budget of Investor	$[900000, 1100000[$
Interest rate	$[0.02, 0.04[$
Discount rate	$[0.01, 0.11[$
Leeway	$[0.05, 0.09[$
Net return of rental	$[0.65, 0.75[$
House loss value	$[0.08, 0.12[$
Margin rate	$[0.02, 0.024[$
Cost Parameter (€/m^2)	$[750, 1000[$
Max Building sites	$[1, 3[$
Number of Bedrooms	$[1, 6[$
House surface : $a + b$(N. of Bedrooms $- 1$)	$a : [18, 31[, a : [24, 33[$
Building time : $8 + BTSup$	$BTSup : [0, 4[$

Table III showcases parameters that are assigned random uniform values to introduce variability and observe its impact on the outcomes. The data sources of this example also include the *PERVAL Database*, a comprehensive dataset produced by the Chamber of Notaries, providing insights into various housing and land metrics, and the *AirDNA*, which is a dataset that offers information related to housing demands and valuations. We also use other Datasets to incorporate *INSEE* (*Institut National de la Statistique et des Études Économiques* is the "*French National Institute of Statistics and Economic Studies*".) data, providing demographic and economic parameters. Others additional datasets include: [20] for building sector data, [21] for commuting costs to the *CBD*, and valuable insights from focus groups with real estate agents and developers.

The outputs obtained from the executable *ABM/LUCC* model allow us to visualise and analyse the dynamics and impacts of interactions between economic agents and the virtual spatialised socio-economic environment. The various policy scenarios highlight the impacts of interventions on urban development and real estate dynamics in Corsica. By meticulously examining developer bankruptcies, market price variations, distances to key landmarks, such as the *Central Business District* (*CBD*) and the beach, as well as the *Mean Seaview Index*, we have gathered useful information on the effects of policy levers. The data generated coupled with appropriate statistical indicators and graphs, enable a better understanding of territorial dynamics of the socio-economic system, identification of emerging trends, and assessment of the impacts of simulated policies and interventions. As an example, we present below the results obtained through the different scenarios concerning the number of bankruptcies and average prices on the two markets. In Figure 6, we observe a pronounced divergence in developer outcomes across the different scenarios. Developer bankruptcies number 2,791 in the *BAU* scenario, surge to 27,333 in the *BTRI* scenario, and show marginal increases or decreases in other scenarios. The *BTRI* scenario precipitates a significant increase in bankruptcies, underscoring the crucial role of tourist rentals in the developer economy. Conversely, scenarios such as the *TTRI* and *CBD-Z* exhibit a comparatively stable or slightly improved environment for developers, indicating a delicate balance between regulatory stringency and market sustainability. As shown in Figure 7, the *LM* exhibits resilience, with minor price fluctuations across scenarios, suggesting a stable market where external influences or policy changes have marginal impacts on land prices (outliers are not displayed.). However, the *BTRI* scenario significantly elevates *HM* prices, indicating a constrained supply amidst unwavering demand. This elevation, a more common economic phenomenon, reflects the pronounced effect of restrictive policies on market dynamics.

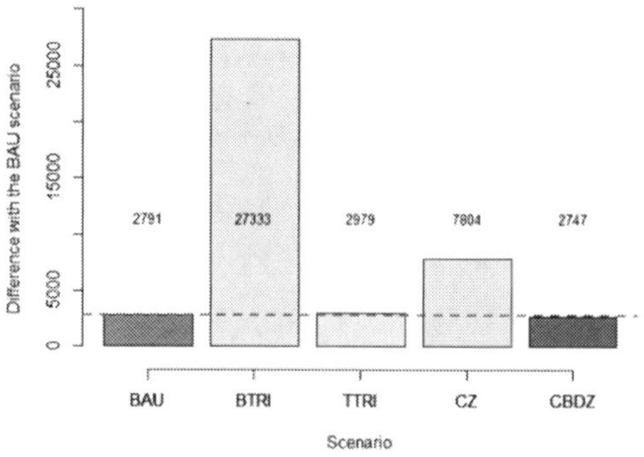

Figure 6. Number of developer bankruptcies by scenario.

V. CONCLUSION AND PERSPECTIVES

The *5-SSIMP* modelling method presented in this paper illustrates a structured and iterative approach to developing modular and reusable *ABM/LUCC*, while facilitating interdisciplinary collaboration. The introduction of *Reusable Building Blocks* (*RBB*) at different stages of the *5-SSIMP* process enhances the modularity, reusability, and robustness of executable *ABM/LUCC* models. The practical example of *ABM/LUCC* applied to the socio-economic tourism system in

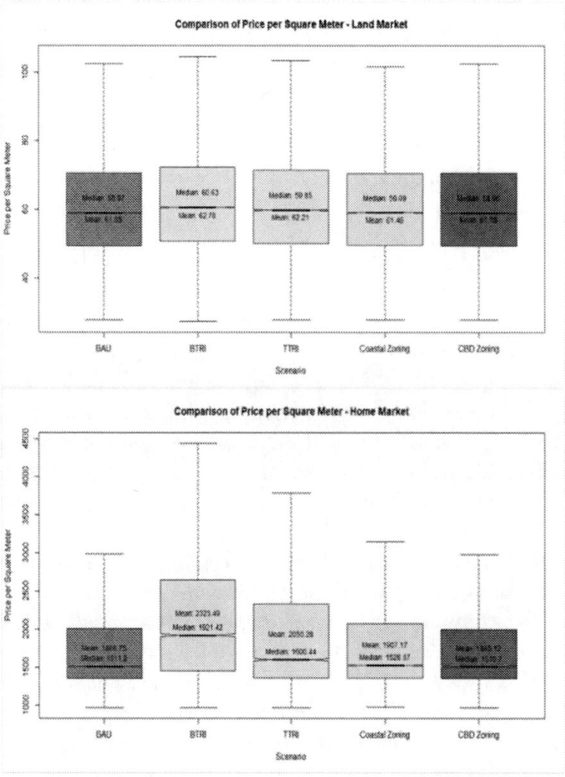

Figure 7. Dispersion of price per square meter for *LM* and *HM*.

Corsica demonstrates the effectiveness of this method, showing how generic conceptual (*conRBB*), computational (*comRBB*), and executable (*exeRBB*) components can be defined, integrated, and implemented. The simulated market dynamics presented as an example reveal complex interactions between economic agents, suggesting valuable insights for analysis and decision-making in Corsica [22]. To continue improving and developing the *5-SSIMP* method and its applications, several research directions will be explored in the coming years. We aim to integrate *Artificial Intelligence* (*AI*) and *Machine Learning* techniques to enhance the predictive and adaptive capabilities of *ABM/LUCC*.

REFERENCES

[1] E. Gamma, R. Helm, R. Johnson, and J. Vlissides, "Design patterns: Abstraction and reuse of object-oriented design", in *ECOOP'93—Object-Oriented Programming: 7th European Conference Kaiserslautern, Germany, July 26–30, 1993 Proceedings 7*, Springer, 1993, pp. 406–431.

[2] M. J. Blas, S. Gonnet, and B. P. Zeigler, "Towards a universal representation of devs: A metamodel-based definition of devs formal specification", in *2021 Annual Modeling and Simulation Conference (ANNSIM)*, IEEE, 2021, pp. 1–12.

[3] L. Jacobson and J. R. G. Booch, *The unified modeling language reference manual*. Addison-Wesley, 2021.

[4] R. Cervenka and I. Trencansky, *The Agent Modeling Language-AML: A Comprehensive Approach to Modeling Multi-Agent Systems*. Springer Science & Business Media, 2007.

[5] V. Grimm *et al.*, "The odd protocol for describing agent-based and other simulation models: A second update to improve clarity, replication, and structural realism", *Journal of Artificial Societies and Social Simulation*, vol. 23, no. 2, 2020.

[6] S. Friedenthal, A. Moore, and R. Steiner, *A practical guide to SysML: the systems modeling language*. Morgan Kaufmann, 2014.

[7] M. Najdek, M. Paciorek, W. Turek, and A. Byrski, "Three new design patterns for scalable agent-based computing and simulation", *Informatica*, vol. 35, no. 2, pp. 379–400, 2024.

[8] M. Rudolph, S. Kurz, and B. Rakitsch, "Hybrid modeling design patterns", *Journal of Mathematics in Industry*, vol. 14, no. 1, p. 3, 2024.

[9] L. Serena, M. Marzolla, G. D'Angelo, and S. Ferretti, "Design patterns for multilevel modeling and simulation", in *2023 IEEE/ACM 27th International Symposium on Distributed Simulation and Real Time Applications (DS-RT)*, IEEE, 2023, pp. 48–55.

[10] D. Vandevoorde and N. M. Josuttis, *C++ Templates: The Complete Guide*. Addison-Wesley Professional, 2002, ISBN: 978-0201734843.

[11] W. B. Arthur, "Complexity and the economy", in *Handbook of Research on Complexity*, Edward Elgar Publishing, 2009.

[12] L. Tesfatsion, "Modeling economic systems as locally-constructive sequential games", *Journal of Economic Methodology*, vol. 24, no. 4, pp. 384–409, 2017.

[13] D. Prunetti *et al.*, "Abm/lucc of a complex economic system of land and home markets facing an intense residential development", in *2021 IEEE Symposium Series on Computational Intelligence (SSCI)*, IEEE, 2021, pp. 1–8.

[14] M. Livermore, "Mr potatohead framework-a software tool for collaborative land-use change modeling", in *Proceedings of the International environmental modelling and software society (iEMSs) 2010 international congress on environmental modelling and software: Modelling for environment's sake, fifth Biennial meeting, Ottawa, Canada.*, 2010, pp. x–x.

[15] D. C. Parker, "An economic perspective on agent-based models of land use and land cover change", in *The Oxford Handbook of Land Economics*, J. Duke and J. Wu, Eds., Oxford University Press, 2014, ch. 16, pp. 402–429.

[16] D. C. Parker, D. G. Brown, J. G. Polhill, P. J. Deadman, and S. M. Manson, "Illustrating a new'conceptual design pattern'for agent-based models of land use via five case studies—the mr potatohead framework", in Universidad de Valladolid, 2008.

[17] D. C. Parker *et al.*, "Mr potatohead: Property market editionl development of a common description template and code base for agent-based land market models", in *Social Simulation Conference 2019, 15th annual Social Simulation Conference*, 2019.

[18] E. Innocenti, C. Detotto, C. Idda, D. C. Parker, and D. Prunetti, "An iterative process to construct an interdisciplinary abm using mr potatohead: An application to housing market models in touristic areas", *Ecological Complexity*, vol. 44, p. 100 882, 2020.

[19] S. Tisue and U. Wilensky, "Netlogo: A simple environment for modeling complexity", in *International conference on complex systems*, Citeseer, vol. 21, 2004, pp. 16–21.

[20] RF, "Plateforme ouverte des données publiques françaises", 2024, [Online]. Available: https://www.data.gouv.fr/ (visited on 08/13/2024).

[21] RF, "Impots.gouv.fr", 2024, [Online]. Available: https://www.impots.gouv.fr/ (visited on 08/13/2024).

[22] D. Prunetti, E. Innocenti, C. Detotto, C. Idda, and L. Yuheng, "Using spatial econometrics models to parametrize ABM : an application to land and housing market in Corsica", in *Séminaire invité du Grupo de Investigación en Dinámica Económica (GIDE)*, Montevideo, Uruguay, Apr. 2022.

Multi-agent Dynamic Interaction in Simulation of Complex Adaptive Systems

Hantao Hua†, Feng Zhu‡*, Yiping Yao‡ and Wenjie Tang‡
† College of Computer, ‡ College of Systems Engineering
National University of Defense Technology
Changsha, China
e-mail: {ht_hua | zhufeng | ypyao | tangwenjie}@nudt.edu.cn

Abstract—**Agent-based modeling and simulation is an effective approach to study complex adaptive systems. With the increasing scale of the simulated system, the interactions between autonomous agents become more and more complex. It is difficult to describe the dynamic interaction between agents by model code intuitively. In addition, the static interaction structure in a multi-agent model leads to long running time and more memory resource consumption. Therefore, this paper proposes a method to graphically describe the dynamic interactions between different agents, named Multi-Agent interaction Graph (MAG). MAG takes agent model class as the basic element of graphical composition. The data communication between agent models is established by using subscribe/publish mechanism, and the interaction between agent model instances is accurately determined based on the dynamic attribute filtering algorithm, which is generated by the large models include Large Language Model (LLM) and Large Vision Model (LVM) automatically from the MAG. The transmission of irrelevant communication data between agent model instances is reduced, and the simulation execution time and memory consumption are reduced. Taking two scenarios as case studies, this paper proves that MAG can model the dynamic interaction between agents, and the execution time of different numbers of agents situation is reduced by 20% - 60%, which can effectively support the scalability of the number of agent model instances. Additional scenario experiments were also conducted to demonstrate the stability and generality of the dynamic attribute filtering algorithm for large model generation.**

Keywords-complex adaptive systems; graphical modeling and simulation; multi-agent interaction; automatic generation of dynamic data filter.

I. INTRODUCTION

Agent based modeling and simulation [1] is an effective approach to study Complex Adaptive Systems (CAS), which is a system composed of autonomous, interacting agents and the interactions between agents will change frequently [2]. With the increasing scale of agents in a CAS, the interactions between agents become more and more complex, showing the characteristics of complex interacting structure and diverse interacting behavior [3]. How to describe the complex dynamic inter-actions between these agents intuitively and how to reduce the interaction overhead in CAS simulation execution bring challenges to traditional multi-agent modeling and simulation approach and environment.

On one hand, it is difficult to describe the dynamic interacions between agents by model code intuitively, because of their complicated interacting structure. The graphical composite modeling method is introduced into multi-agent modeling and simulation, which can simplify the CAS modeling and greatly shorten the development time. Graphical composite modeling method has a higher level of abstraction than code and is closer to the problem domain [4]. Beginners or experienced users can intuitively and efficiently compose simpler models through mouse dragging in a visual user interface to create more complex models and shield the details of code programming such as parallel computing, simulation synchronization, and event scheduling in this process, so as to effectively reduce the difficulty of modeling CAS.

On the other hand, with the increasing of the complexity of the simulated system, the number of the agents will grow, and the communication between the agent models will also increase [5]. The execution time of the complex composite model is usually very long, which limits the scalability of the multi-agent system scale [6]. Even in some special cases, the multi-agent CAS model cannot be executed at all, due to the growth of communication. At present, the complex interactive communication between multi-agent models is mostly limited to a few specific simulation scenarios or reduces the accuracy of the model of CAS. In addition, the existing multi-agent interactive filtering methods are often carried out for specific problems, and there is a lack of a general filtering method, takes time and effort to generate an algorithm for each filtering method.

This paper proposes a multi-agent graphical composite modeling method, named MAG, which takes the agent model as the basic graphical element of the CAS multi-agent model, and establishes the data communication between the agent models by means of public/subscribe. In the actual running process of simulation, the dynamic attribute filtering algorithm is used to filter the non-interactive data between agent models, to build a dynamic agent interaction network. It reduces the transmission of irrelevant communication between agent models, and thus reduce the simulation execution time and memory consumption. The main contribution of this paper is to support multi-agent dynamic interaction in CAS from two aspects. One is graphical modeling and the other is communication data filtering.

(1) The MAG, a graphical composite modeling method, is proposed to solve the complexity of modeling multi-agent dynamic interaction, which is more intuitive than code written by general programming language.

(2) With the MAG modeling method, a dynamic attribute filtering algorithm is introduced to reduce the problem of long simulation time and resource consumption caused by irrelevant communication data transmission between agent model instances. Considering the generality of dynamic attribute filtering algorithm, we use Large Language Models (LLM) to implement

the transformation of filtering methods in MAG to C++ code.

The structure of this paper is as follows. Section II introduces the related work. Section III introduces multi-agent interacion graph. Section IV introduces the general data filtering mechanism generated by the large model. In the Section V, we take the multi-aircraft collision avoidance scenario and swarm robots cooperation scenario as examples, proved that MAG modeling method can effectively support the dynamic interaction modeling between agents of CAS, also proved the stability and scalability of our method. Finally, our conclusion will be made with an indication of the future work.

II. Background and Related work

In terms of graphical modeling approach, Petri net [7] constructs a network structure through Place, Transition, Token and other basic elements to analyze the structure of the system. At present, Petri net is constantly developing forward. For example, Aalst et al. [8] proposed a strategy of modeling complex processes based on hierarchical colored Petri net. Staines et al. [9] proposed the method of transforming UML sequence diagram into Petri net, to make use of its rigorous model verification method. Drakaki et al. [10] proposed a dynamic resource allocation method by combin-ing the colored Petri net and agent-based control system. Tang et al. [11] proposed a hierarchical Petri net modeling paradigm to build an aerial collision avoidance model under multi-aircraft scenario. Jamal et al. [12] extended the agent-based mobile Petri net to simulate the mobility, concurrency, and distribution of agents. Hsieh [13] combined multi-agent architecture and Petri net to solve the problem of distributed dynamic scheduling of hospital patients. However, the current Petri net does not support to describe the dynamic interactions between autonomous multi-agent.

Event Graph is a graphical modeling paradigm of discrete events. In order to improve the composability of event graph, Buss et al. [14] introduced the object-oriented modeling ideas on the basis of the event graph modeling paradigm, and proposed the concept of the Listener Event Graph Ob-jects (LEGO). PEG extended the basic event graph to support graphical composite modeling of discrete event simulation models [15]. Barclay et al. [16] proposed the dynamic chain event graph, which can be combined with Semi-Markov chains. However, the extension and optimization of the above event graph modeling paradigms mostly adopt static interaction structure, which leads to more running time and more resource consumption in a multi-agent model.

Zeigler proposed the Discrete Event System Specification (DEVS) [17]. The DEVS specification contains two types of paradigms, the atomic model paradigm for describing the actual models with specific logical functions, and the coupled model paradigm for building existing atomic models into more complex models. In addition, Hamri et al. [18] introduced minimum/maximum delay into the transition function to extend DEVS for the hardware simulation modeling. Camus et al. [19] combined DEVS specification and multi-agent modeling method to solve the problem of multi-model modeling and simulation of complex systems. Kulakowski et al. [20]adopted the DEVS theory to build a multi-agent system, which was used to simulate the crowd evacuation process when a fire occurred. Jarrah et al. [21]studied the interaction behavior modeling among multiple agents based on the DEVS framework. However, the above extension of DEVS theory does not consider the requirements of reducing multi-agent communication consumption.

Similarly, Markovian agents model is a modeling technique for analyzing large-scale distributed interactive systems. In this model, each agent is treated as a continuous time Markov chain (CTMC) whose behavior is influenced by interactions with other agents [22]. Therefore, the focus of the model is naturally placed on the state itself and the transition probability between states, rather than the dynamic interaction process behind the state transition. Multiformalism modeling approach combines multiple modeling languages and tools to deal with different aspects of complex systems [23]. It pays more attention to the coordination of paradigm, so it is suitable for those complex systems that are difficult to be fully described by a single modeling language, rather than focusing on the dynamic change process of the interaction process between states.

Hybrid hierarchical modeling theory combines models with different description specifications to realize hierarchical hybrid modeling of complex systems. The Ptolemy system developed by Berkeley University [24]was designed under this theory. The Ptolemy model was described by using a Finite State Machine (FSM) with ports. Each state in Ptolemy can also be described by a FSM with ports, to support the construction of application system in a hierarchical way [25]. Flexible Analysis, Modeling and Exercise System (FLAMES) [26] is a commercial hierarchical simulation integration environment, which supports systems and engineering analysis, test and evaluation, training, mission planning and deduction, etc. MathWorks [27]proposed a hybrid dynamic modeling method based on the combination of Simulink and state flow. However, Ptolemy, FLAMES and Simulink were difficult to solve the problem of long running time and more resource consumption caused by irrelevant communication data transmission between multi-agent models.

In the aspect of dynamic interaction modeling, dynamic structure [28] is listed as one of the key challenges of co-simulation, which can be used to study self-organizing cluster system. Uhrmacher [29] constructed a formal theory based on that DEVS is independent to the specific implementation to support the model to adapt to its own interaction structure and behavior and implemented this theory on the James platform. Barros [30] proposed a formal theory, HFSS, which aims to represent hierarchical and modular hybrid systems with dynamic structures. HFSS is a framework for merging components built in different patterns so that a more efficient and easier to understand model can be constructed by changing the structure of the network. Dormido [31] considered the modeling problem of variable-structure hybrid power system. By proposing a new algorithm and using the existing object-oriented hybrid system modeling language, the model was transformed into a model suitable for description and simulation. Hu [32] specifically discussed the capabilities of the variable structure, structure change, and interface change in the modeling and simulation environment based on DEVS. They discussed the operation of structure change and interface change, and defined the operating boundaries respectively. Most of the above variable-structure modeling methods are based on DEVS or DEVS-like theory, which can describe the dynamic interaction process of multi-agents, but they lack consideration for the optimization of data communication among multi-agents. Fishwick [33] defines hyper-modeling as a general theory for linking system models and their components, but hyper-model is more concerned with interactions within the model, between different models, and between people and models. As the complexity of the model is increased with the increasing complexity of the actual system, which often results in a long simulation time. Mehlhase [34] proposed a framework for modeling and simulating the variable structure models by using hybrid decomposition method in general simulation environment. This method integrates three tools including Dymola, OpenModelica and Matlab/Simulink, and solved the problem of long simulation time by changing the set of equations during simulation running, which reduces the accuracy of CAS models. In addition, the existing multi-agent interactive filtering methods are often carried out for specific problems, and there is a lack of a general filtering method, takes time and effort to generate an algorithm for each filtering method.

Large language models has advanced remarkably in recent years with the advent of pretrained Transformers [35] such as BERT [36] and GPT [37]. With its scaled to hundreds of billions of parameters and started to display early signs of artificial general intelligence, their applications have also transcended text processing, also attempts to bridge the gap between natural langauge processing (NLP) domain and simulation domain on the topic of LLMs applications. LLMs and in-context learning have been applied to code-generation tasks. Chain-of-Thought (CoT) prompting [38], where a language model is prompted with in-context examples of inputs, chain-of-thought rationales (a series of intermediate reasoning steps), and outputs, has shown impressive abilities for solving structured output problems like code-generation tasks. While CoT relies on the ability of LLMs to both generate a reasoning path and execute it, it is not yet possible to translate the agent interaction diagram directly into the executable code. However, although the traditional method can directly convert the agent interaction diagram into code, it needs to be re-modeled for each task and cannot be generalized to general tasks.

The limitation of LLM is that it can only deal with plain text type data and cannot deal with more complex multimodal data types. The task requirements in the field of computer vision are similar to those in the field of natural language processing, and the algorithm of instruction adjustment can be introduced into the field of computer vision or multimodal tasks. LLaVA [39] is an end-to-end trained large-scale multimodal model that connects a visual encoder and a language model for multimodal tasks such as general vision and language understanding.

In a word, in addition to the above current related work, a new method is needed. On one hand, it solves the problem of modeling complexity of dynamic interaction between agents intuitively. On the other hand, it solves the problem of long running time and more memory consumption caused by irrelevant communication data transmission of dayamic interacion. In addition, the generality and efficiency of the new method should be guaranteed.

III. Multi-agent Interaction Graph

The MAG is designed to support the modeling of the dynamic interaction between agents. It uses the agent model class instead of agent model instance as the basic graphical modeling element. An attribute filter should be configured between each pair of agent model class. After the graphical multi-agent model is built, it will be automatically translated into the executable model of *LP* (Logical Process) paradigm. During the simulation execution time, the agent model instances are generated dynamically according to the simulation scenario, and the interaction between the agent instances is determined dynamically based on the calculation results of the attribute filter.

A. Graphical Representation of Agent Model

To describe the agent model graphically, a port diagram is used to represent the agent model class, as shown in Figure 1. The ports in the diagram are mainly responsible for establishing the communication channel between agent models. The port *p1* represents the input port of the agent model, and the port *p2* represents the output port of the agent model. The behavior logic of the agent model can be graphically represented as an extended Petri Net [40]. The $data$ components are used to store the state data of the agent model. The state data can be used as the input data to a $function$ component. The $function$ components are employed to indicate the computing functions, which changes the state data of the agent model.. The $link$ component is used to represent the control flow and the data flow. A directed arc from $data$ component to $function$ component means the data component is an input of the $function$ component. A directed arc from $function$ component to $data$ component means the data component is an output of the $function$ component.

To facilitate users to understand the structure provided by the agent model, it is necessary to provide the metadata information of the agent model class, as shown in the right side of Figure 1. *ClassName* represents the class name of the agent model, and each agent model will be automatically transformed into a C++ class. *AttributeList* denotes the set of state variables of the agent model. *EventList* represents the set of events in the agent model. The processing of each event will cause the agent state to change instantaneously. *PortList* denotes the port set of the agent model for external interaction. The agent model can communicate with other agent models through input/output port. *MapList* represents the set of the pair $< event, port >$. The processing of an event in an agent will not only change its own state, but also trigger an interaction between the agent model and another agent models. The interaction here is

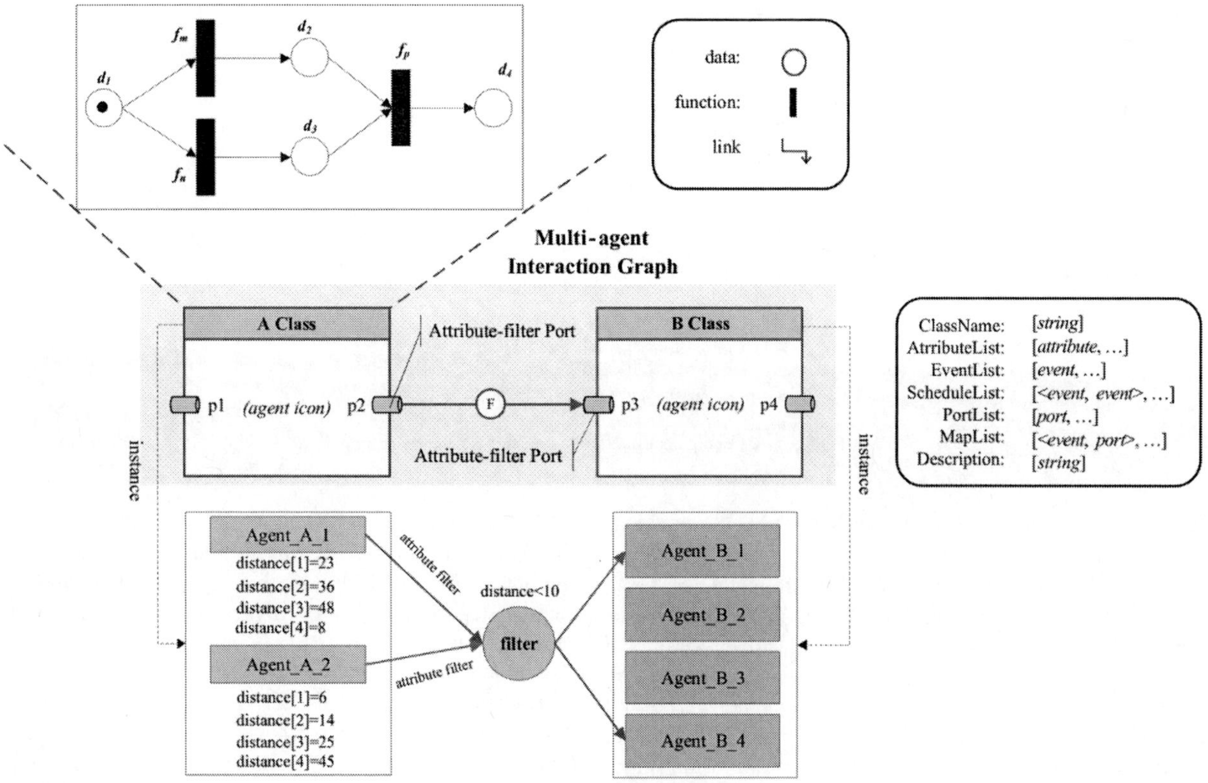

Figure 1. Graphical representation of an agent model and its interacion.

realized through port communication. Description represents the behavior rules.

B. Structure of Multi-agent Interaction Graph

MAG describes the dynamic interaction between agent model instances shown in Figure 1. The connection with attribute filter F between the ports of two agent models *Agent_A* and *Agent_B* indicates that there may be interactions between them. The attribute filter can also not be configured, which means that there is always interaction between the two agent models. Before the simulation execution, the attribute filtered expression set should be configured on the attribute filter F. Several filtered expressions can be established for the same attribute of the agent model. The filtered expression establishes the criterion of pass/reject on the attribute. To pass a filter, at least one filtered expression in that filter should be satisfied. Only by passing a certain attribute filtered expression configured by the agent model, it is considered that the interaction conditions between the agent model instance and the corresponding agent model instance can be satisfied, so as to realize the communication between the agent instances. In the process of simulation execution, several instances of the agent model class will be generated, and the interaction between specific agent model instances is determined by the attribute filter F.

As shown in Figure 1, the agent model class *Agent_A* connects with the agent model class *Agent_B*, which indicates that the instance of agent model class *Agent_A* perhaps interact with the instances of agent model *Agent_B*. It is supposed that there are two instances of class *Agent_A* and four instances of class *Agent_B* will be generated according to the simulation scenario. The communication from the agent model instances of the class *Agent_A* to the agent model instances of the class *Agent_B* is determined by the attribute filtered expression $distance < 10$ which is configured on the filter. Supposing that the positions of all the agent model instances of class *Agent_B* remains unchanged, when the position of the agent model instances of class *Agent_A* is updated, the variable distance will be calculated. Therefore, by checking whether the expression $distance < 10$ is true, which two agent moddel instance can communicate with each other is dtermined. For example, the model instance *Agent_A_1* is able to interact the model instance *Agent_B_4*. Similarly, the model instance *Agent_A_2* is able to interact to the model instance *Agent_B_1*.

IV. Automatic Filter generation

An agent model can be described as an extended Petri net [40], each place is used to store the state variables of the agent model, and each transition is always labeled by an event. The dynamic interaction between the agents can be modelled by MAG. In order to enable the execution of a CAS model on existing Discrete Event Simulation (DES) platforms, we map

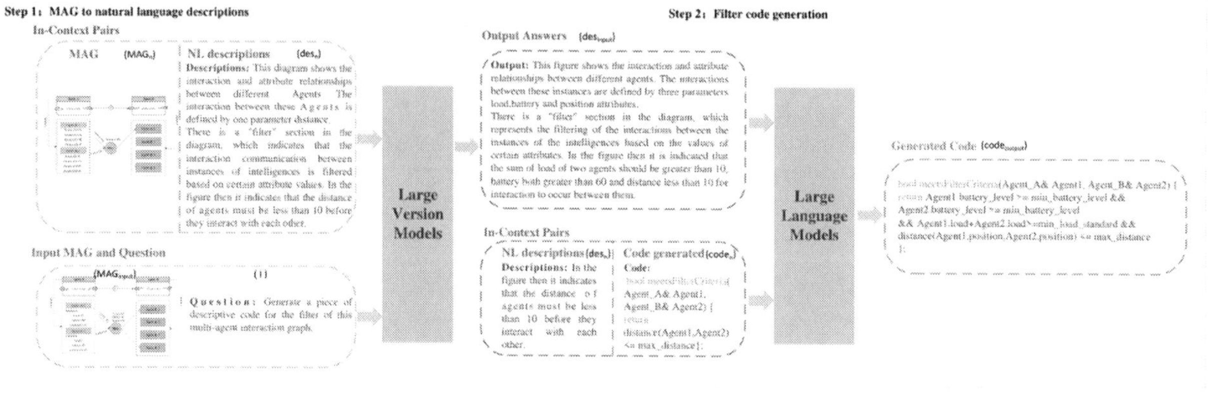

Figure 2. Dynamic data filtering automated generation process.

an agent to a *LP* and mapping the interactions between agents to update attributes between *LPs* [41].

Previous work has implemented the transformation of Agent elements from MAG diagrams to code, in the process of translating MAG to DES code, we search all the graphical elements and convert the graphical element into discrete event simulation code. For each agent model element, we build a *LP* class in C++ object-oriented language. An agent model is translated into a *LP* class which is composed of an initial method, several event procedures, and a series of variables. Each initial method sets the initial value for the variables of the *LP* and then schedule some necessary events for simulation execution. A *LP* changes the values of the variables that describe the agent state through processing events. For each filter element, it is needed to search for all agents associated with a filter and make a connection with them. After that, in the simulation execution, the code for scheduling interactive events will be executed according to the calculation of the filtered expression in the filter.

It is not easy to implement the attribute filtering method in MAG and the parameter in agent into code expressions, especially considering that there may be many different expressions of MAG in practical applications. It is difficult to find a general filter code expression generation method. The generation of filters is often closely related to the content presented in MAG. LVM can describe the information presented in MAG as natural language, but LVM does not perform well on natural language code generation tasks. Similarly, some common LLMS work well for the task of generating code in natural language, but do not take pictures as their input. For the text of these given output styles of code, because of the hallucination of LLM, the direct use of LLM to generate will bring a certain chance of misformatted output. In-Context Learning (ICL) is brought to reduce the probability of hallucination, that is, several input-output generation examples are placed on the input side, and then the problem description and input are used as prompt for LLM/LVM. This has proven to be an efficient means of structural text generation based on LLM/LVM [42].

We use large models (including LLMs and LVMs) and CoT Prompting to convert MAG into filter code expressions. Given the picture form of MAG, we break the problem down into a step-by-step form based on CoT prompt, as follows: LVM based on ICL is used to convert MAG into text description close to natural language, including input parameters and discriminant logic of filter expression, and LLM is used to convert generated natural language into corresponding filter code. The context and CoT prompt process is shown in Figure 2. In Figure 2, for the MAG shown in Figure 1, first complete the generation of in-context examples of MAG-description on the manually configured MAG sample set as prompt input to the LVM. The description for filter generating the code of MAG is obtained, includes the input parameters and the discriminant logic of the code. The same ICL method is used in the LLM generation code phase, merging LVM generated descriptions with in-context examples as prompt input to the LLM. These examples are manually written and can typically be constructed without an accompanying graph. Then, it will generate a program (right of Figure 2) that can be executed which is based on the input MAG(s) to perform the described filter task.

$$LVM(I, pairs < MAG_1, des_1 >, pairs < MAG_2, des_2 >, \\ \cdots, pairs < MAG_n, des_n >, MAG_{input}) \rightarrow des_{input} \quad (1)$$

$$LLM(I, pairs < des_1, code_1 >, pairs < des_2, code_2 >, \\ \cdots, pairs < des_n, code_n >, des_{input}) \rightarrow code_{output} \quad (2)$$

We showed in (1) and (2) for the process of generating code from MAG using LLM in combination with LVM. Here, $pairs\langle x, y\rangle$ is the ICL to identifie the example MAG-description pair or description-code pair, as shown in the in-context pairs above step 1 in Figure 2. Where I represents the definition of the task, MAG_{input} represents the input we want to get the result, as shown input MAG and question below step 1 in Figure 2. des_{input} represents the intermediate module

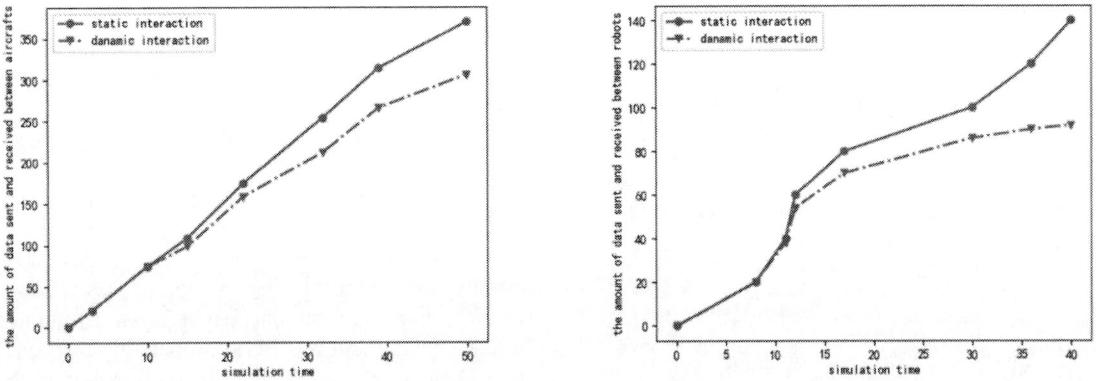

(a) Aircraft Collision Avoidance Scenario
(b) Swarm robots Cooperation Scenario

Figure 3. The total amount of communication data.

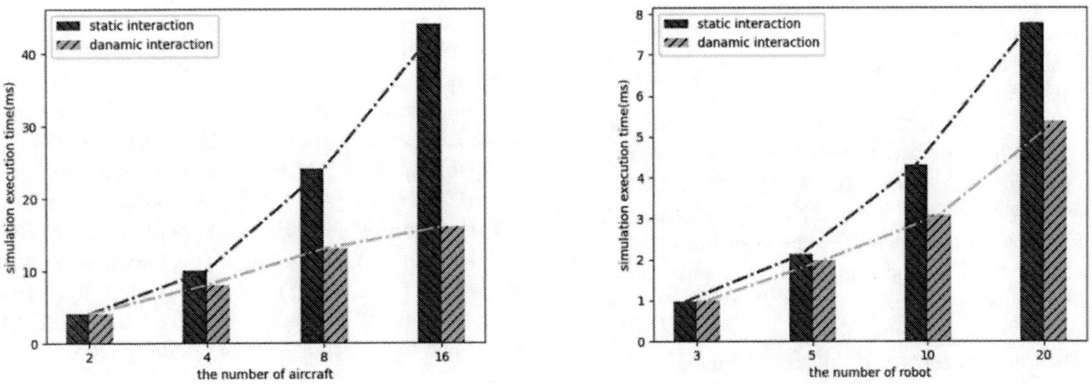

(a) Aircraft Collision Avoidance Scenario
(b) Swarm robots Cooperation Scenario

Figure 4. Execution time of MAG-based model.

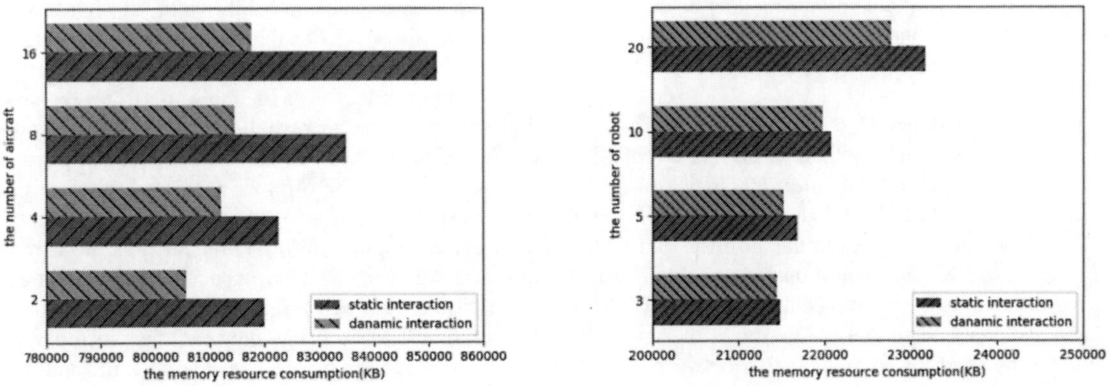

(a) Aircraft Collision Avoidance Scenario
(b) Swarm robots Cooperation Scenario

Figure 5. Memory consumption of the MAG-based model.

for filter code generation, the same way to generate the filter code we end up with like step 1, we can get the result code $code_{output}$.

V. Experiments and Analysis

Our work provides a general, efficient and scalable multi-agent simulation framework. We test some typical application scenarios of multi-agent simulation, including aircraft collision avoidance scenario with less inter-agent communication interaction and robot collaboration scenario with more frequent inter-agent communication interaction. We now describe these scenarios, their evaluation settings, and their results for analyzing.

A. Test Scenarios Introduction

Aircraft Collision Avoidance Scenarios. In the airspace near the civil airport, with the increasing of airspace density, collision avoidance between aircraft is considered to be a key problem affecting flight safety. Because the time of aircraft collision is very short, it is necessary to predict the flight path of the aircraft as soon as possible to detect the possible collision risk, so as to guarantee the multi-aircraft flight. Agent-based modeling and simulation is very suitable for analyzing multi-aircraft collision avoidance scenarios. In this paper, we assume that (1) before any two aircraft enter the adjacent airspace, there is no need to exchange position data between aircraft; (2) the height of the collision cylinder which are twice as long as the vertical size of the aircraft; and (3) two aircraft may collide when they are encountering each other at a certain angle, and they will not collide again after the collision is released. Under this assumption, the modeling for multi-aircraft collision avoidance in this scenario involves the following interactions: (1)when any two aircraft enter the adjacent airspace, there may be collision between them. In order to avoid collision, these aircraft often need to exchange position data and adjust the corresponding flight direction and angle in time; and (2) when any two aircraft are free of collision risk, the position data sharing between aircraft can be cancelled to reduce the communication between aircraft models.

This paper takes Tang-Piera multi-aircraft collision problem [43] as a segggd on GMAS, to verify the running time, memory cost and scalability of the model based on the MAG modeling method and the dynamic attribute filtering algorithm based on LLMs.

We use three agent model classes to build a four-aircraft collision avoidance model. Since there is no risk of collision avoidance between *aircraft0* and *aircraft3*, they can be instantiated by the same agent model class *AircraftA*. The only difference between them is their initial position and speed. *aircraft1* is generated by the agent model class *AircraftB* and *aircraft2* is generated by the agent model class *AircraftC*. Since the collision avoidance logic in each aircraft is the same, the same filter can be used for communication between aircraft. Its filter expression can be set to horizontal $distance < 88$ m, which also means that when the horizontal distance between two aircraft is within this range, the position information of the other aircraft will be sent or received. Therefore, a multi-aircraft dynamic interaction model is constructed graphically through GMAS.

Swarm robots cooperation Scenarios. In search and rescue environments, swarm robots are often used to locate people or transport materials. These robots often have different functions, such as sonar detection, infrared thermal imaging and robotic arm operation, they collaborate with each other to complete more complex tasks. Since the scene is often more complex and difficult to predict, multi-agent modeling and simulation of robot behavior has become a feasible and efficient way. In this paper, we assume that (1) there are three kinds of robots in the scenario, which have the functions of sonar detection, infrared thermal imaging and robotic arm operation respectively; (2) all sonar detection and infrared thermal imaging robots will search after receiving the search task, and if they find trapped people, they will cooperate with the robotic arm operator to complete the rescue task; and (3)each probe robot works with a maximum of one arm-operated robot. Under this assumption, the modeling for swarm cooperative robots in this scenario involves the following interactions: (1)when the probe robot finds the trapped person, it will look for and cooperate with the nearest robotic arm robot that is free and meets the demand of power and load, which requires the information interaction and communication between the probe robot and all robotic arm robots; and (2)when the probe robot finds the robot arm that works with it, the data sharing between the robots is no longer required for reducing the communication between robot models. Similarly, we use GMAS [40] environment and implement the dynamic attribute filtering algorithm at the swarm robots cooperation scenarios to verify the running time, memory cost and scalability of the model based on the MAG modeling method and the dynamic attribute filtering algorithm based on LLMs.

We use three agent model classes to build a swarm robots cooperation rescue model, since there is no needs for communication between each kinds of robots, each kinds of robots can be instantiated by one agent model class like *RobotA*. The only difference between them is their pamameters like location, remain power, etc. The probability of a "life-form found" event is poisson distributed as the robot keeps searching when no result is found. The probability of "finding a life form" event is Poisson distributed. After finding a life form, the probe robot will search for the nearest eligible robot arm to cooperate in the rescue mission. Since the same interaction parameters are required for each type of probe robot and robotic arm robot in the process of seeking cooperation, the same communication filter can be applied. Information, such as the current status, remaining power and load capacity of the robot is filtered. When the above conditions of the two robots meet the standard, the location data exchange between the two robots is started to achieve collaborative rescue. Figure 2 illustrates the large model-based MAG-to-filter code generation process for the swarm robot collaboration scenario. The generated code will be directly used in the discriminative expression of the filter.

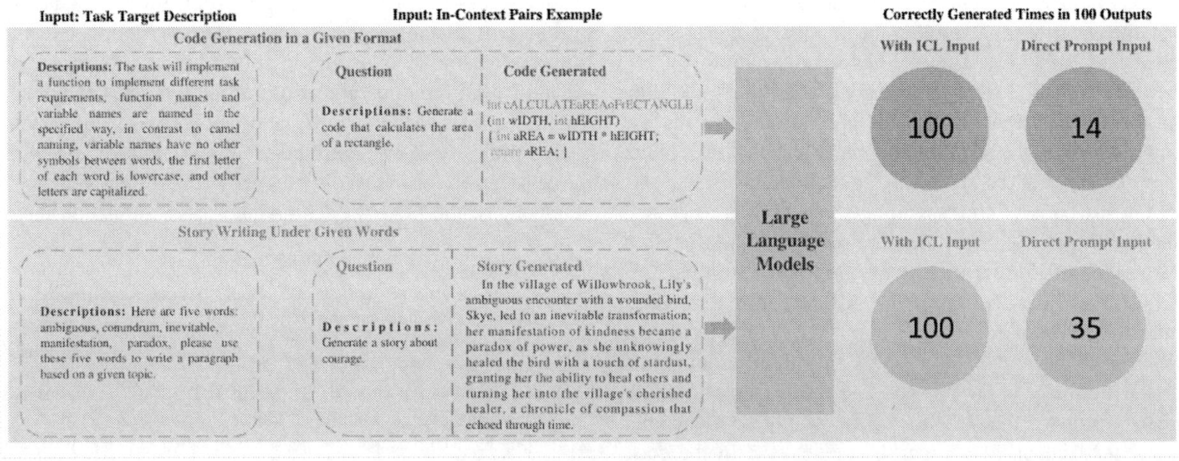

Figure 6. Dynamic data filtering automated generation process.

B. Scenarios Realization Analysis

Aircraft Collision Avoidance Scenarios. We simulated the collision scenario of Tang-Piera four-aircraft in a very short period of time. Four aircraft were both into the adjacent airspace, and successively entered the scene of *collision 1*, *collision 2* and *collision 3*. When the simulation time $T \in [0, 2]$, each two of the four aircraft are in the adjacent airspace, they need to share position data with each other to determine whether they are in collision with an aircraft. When the simulation time $T \in [3, 10]$, *aircraft 0* and *aircraft 1* will encounter the *collision 1*, they will continue to share position data.When the simulation $T > 10$, the *collision 1* is released, and the interaction between them can be cancelled dynamically. When the simulation time $T \in [15, 22]$, *aircraft 0* and *aircraft 2* will encounter the *collision 2*, and they need to continue to maintain interaction.When the simulation $T > 22$, the *collision 2* is released, and the interaction between them can be dynamically disconnected. When the simulation time $T \in [32, 39]$, *aircraft 2* and *aircraft 3* will encounter the *collision 3*, and they need to continue to maintain interaction. When the simulation time $T \in [40, 50]$, the *collision 3* threat is removed, and the four aircraft return to the predetermined trajectory to continue to fly, and the interaction between *aircraft 2* and *aircraft 3* can be cancelled dynamically. We can see that the altitude difference between the two aircraft will collide within [0,10].

Figure 3(a) compares the amount of communication data sent and received between aircraft in two different situations of static interaction (SI, data interaction is always maintained during simulation execution) and dynamic interaction (DI, when the collision is released, the interaction between them can be disconnected dynamically). We can find that when the simulation execution is finished, the total amount of communication between the four aircraft is reduced by 17%.
Swarm robots cooperation Scenarios. We also simulated the swarm robots cooperation scenario in a period of time. Ten robots of each type are initialized to move randomly on a given map, their power gradually decreases with its working time. When the simulation time starts, each robot performs its own detection task separately and does not need to communicate with each other. While a probe robot detects a life form, information such as position and load is shared with idle robotic arm robots in the area with power above a threshold instead of sharing it as a broadcast to reduce data communication. The detecting robot selects the nearest robot that meets the load requirements to cooperate and no longer shares data information with other robots. The above two scenarios are repeated until the task is completed. Figure 3(b) shows the total amount of data communicated under the static and dynamic interaction algorithms. It can be clearly seen that the amount of communication data generated by the dynamic interaction using the filtering-based algorithm produces a significant decrease, and more so as the simulation time progresses, reaching 34% of the optimized amount of communication data at the end of the simulation.

C. Scalability, Stability and generality of our system

Figure 4 compares the execution time of MAG-based model under two different situations, one is static interaction and the other is dynamic interaction. With the increasing of the number of agent, the simulation running time increases when the interaction is not disconnected. When the interaction is disconnected dynamically, the execution time of multi-agent model in 2-16 aircraft situation is reduced by 20%-60% compared with the former, and the execution time of multi-agent model in swarm robot cooperation scenario reduced by approximately 30%. Figure 5 compares the memory resource consumption of the MAG-based model under two different situations: static interaction and dynamic interaction. With the increasing of the number of agent, the consumption of model memory resources of multi-agent model in 2-16 aircraft situation is reduced by 1.8%-4%, and is reduced by 0.8%-5.5% in swarm robot cooperation scenario. That's because the sharing data is only position data(x,y) in this multi-aircraft collistion avoidance model and more attribute data needs to share in the swarm robot model. In summary, it is can be concluded that MAG-based model has good scalability.

The results obtained from large model-based methods often bring problems of interpretability and consistency, and the use of ICL will enhance the stability and consistency of the results. For several simple fixed-style text generation tasks, we use description-text pairs of corresponding styles as ICL pairs, and test whether the results meet the requirements, while using a non-ICL approach (direct input of prompt) as a comparison. Figure 6 shows a description of the different text generation tasks, the ICL pairs used, and the number of times the target text was correctly generated over 100 tests with different inputs. The test environment is Qwen2-7B. The results show that ICL can greatly improve the stability of the output results under the text generation task, so it can be better used in the code generation task under the given format required in this paper.

We also evaluated the accuracy of the filter code generation, constructing different forms of MAG with filter execution logic for validation. To verify the stability and generality of our algorithm, we tested the filter code generation results using different combinations of large models (LLaVa [39]+LLaMa3 [44] and Qwen-VL [45]+Qwen2 [46]), while ablation experiments were performed to verify the necessity of implementing the model architecture in this way. We tested the filter code generation effect with LLaVa+LLaMa3, Qwen-VL+Qwen2 and LVM-only on 100 randomly generated MAGs (manually filtered to ensure the diversity of scenarios and filtering mechanisms), and the test results are shown in Table I.

TABLE I. NUMBER OF SUCCESSFUL FILTER CODE GENERATION FOR DIFFERENT MODELS COMBINATION

Large models (portfolios) used	Successful generation number
LLaVa+LLaMa3	78
Qwen-VL+Qwen2	74
LLaVa-only	17

Here, "successful generation" means that the generated code can be directly used in the filter and realizes the correct filtering function, which shows the stability and generality of the combined filter code generation algorithm using LLM and LVM.

VI. CONCLUSION AND FUTURE WORK

Multi-agent modeling and simulation is an effective means to study complex adaptive system. The traditional static interaction structure leads to the long running time and resource consumption, then this paper proposes a MAG modeling method to graphically describe the dynamic interaction between agent models. In MAG, the communication between agent models is established by using publish/subscribe, and the interaction between agent instances is accurately determined based on the dynamic attribute filtering algorithm. The aircraft collision avoidance experiments in multi-aircraft scenario and the swarm robots cooperation scenario show that MAG can model the dynamic interaction between agents of CAS, reduce the transmission of irrelevant communication data between multi-agent instances, and reduce the simulation execution time and resource consumption. In addition, it shows good scalability. Different combinations of large models and ablation tests have proven the stability and versatility of the system.

In future work, we will build more complex simulation models based on GMAS to verify the effectiveness and efficiency of the MAG-based modeling and simulation method.

REFERENCES

[1] L. F. M. Bristow and K. W. Hipel, "Agent-based modeling of competitive and cooperative behavior under conflict", *IEEE Transactions on Systems, Man, and Cybernetics: Systems*, vol. 44, no. 7, pp. 834–850, 2014.

[2] C. M. Macal and M. J. North, "Tutorial on agent-based modelling and simulation", *Journal of Simulation*, vol. 4, no. 3, pp. 151–162, 2010.

[3] R. Dekkers, "Complex adaptive systems", *Applied Systems Theory*, pp. 211–233, 2017.

[4] T. T. M. Haeusler and J. Kessler, "Chronosphere: A graph based emf model repository for it landscape models", *Software and System Modeling*, vol. 18, no. 4, pp. 1–40, 2019.

[5] R. M. Fujimoto, "Research challenges in parallel and distributed simulation", *ACM Transactions on Modeling and Computer Simulation (TOMACS)*, vol. 26, no. 1, pp. 1–29, 2016.

[6] A. Rousset, B. Herrmann, C. Lang, and L. Philippe, "A survey on parallel and distributed multi-agent systems for high performance computing simulations", *Computer Science Review*, vol. 22, pp. 27–46, 2016.

[7] J. Haas, "Stochastic petri nets for modeling and simulation", in *Proceedings of the 2004 Winter Simulation Conference*, 2004, pp. 101–112.

[8] W. Aalst, C. Stahl, and M. Westergaard, "Strategies for modeling complex processes using colored petri nets", in *Transactions on Petri Nets and Other Models of Concurrency VII* (Lecture Notes in Computer Science), Lecture Notes in Computer Science. Springer, 2013, vol. 7480, pp. 6–55.

[9] S. Staines, "Transforming uml sequence diagrams into petri net", *Journal of Communication and Computer*, vol. 10, no. 1, pp. 72–81, 2013.

[10] M. Drakaki and P. Tzionas, "Modeling and performance evaluation of an agent-based warehouse dynamic resource allocation using colored petri nets", *International Journal of Computer Integrated Manufacturing*, vol. 29, no. 7, pp. 736–753, 2015.

[11] J. Tang and F. Zhu, "Graphical modelling and analysis software for state space-based optimization of discrete event systems", *IEEE Access*, vol. 6, pp. 1–15, 2018.

[12] M. Jamal and N. Zafar, "Extending agent-based mobile petri nets with access control", in *2017 IEEE International Conference on Communication, Computing and Digital Systems (C-CODE)*, IEEE, 2017, pp. 133–138.

[13] F. Hsieh, "A hybrid and scalable multi-agent approach for patient scheduling based on petri net models", *Applied Intelligence*, vol. 47, no. 4, pp. 1–19, 2017.

[14] A. Buss and C. Blais, "Composability and component-based discrete event simulation", in *Proceedings of the 2007 Winter Simulation Conference*, 2007, pp. 694–702.

[15] B. Wang, B. Deng, and F. Xing, "Partitioned event graph: Formalizing lp-based modelling of parallel discrete-event simulation", *Mathematical and Computer Modelling of Dynamical Systems*, vol. 21, no. 2, pp. 153–179, 2014.

[16] L. Barclay, R. Collazo, J. Smith, *et al.*, "The dynamic chain event graph", *Electronic Journal of Statistics*, vol. 9, no. 2, pp. 2130–2169, 2015.

[17] B. P. Zeigler, G. Kim, and H. Praehofer, *Theory of modeling and simulation: integrating discrete event and continuous complex dynamic systems*. Academic Press, 2003.

[18] A. Hamri, N. Giambiasi, and C. Frydman, "Min-max-devs modeling and simulation", *Simulation Modelling Practice and Theory*, vol. 14, pp. 909–929, 2017.

[19] B. Camus, C. Bourjot, and V. Chevrier, "Combining devs with multi-agent concepts to design and simulate multi-models of complex systems", in *2015 Symposium on Theory of Modeling & Simulation: DEVS Integrative M&S Symposium (DEVS)*, IEEE, 2015, pp. 85–90.

[20] A. Kulakowski and B. Rogala, "Agent devs simulation of the evacuation process from a commercial building during a fire", in *2017 Conference on Computer Science and Information Technologies (CSIT)*, IEEE, 2017, pp. 270–279.

[21] M. Jarrah, B. Zeigler, C. Xu, *et al.*, "A multi-agent simulation framework to support agent interactions under different domains", in *2015 18th Asia Pacific Symposium on Intelligent and Evolutionary Systems (IES)*, IEEE, 2015, pp. 211–223.

[22] A. Bobbio, D. Cerotti, M. Gribaudo, M. Iacono, and D. Manini, "Markovian agent models: A dynamic population of interdependent markovian agents", in *Seminal Contributions to Modelling and Simulation: 30 Years of the European Council of Modelling and Simulation*, K. Al-Begain and A. Bargiela, Eds. Cham: Springer International Publishing, 2016, pp. 185–203, ISBN: 978-3-319-33786-9. DOI: 10.1007/978-3-319-33786-9_13.

[23] J. Yang, H. Peng, W. Zhou, J. Zhang, and Z. Wu, "A modular approach for dynamic modeling of multisegment continuum robots", *Mechanism and Machine Theory*, vol. 165, p. 104 429, 2021, ISSN: 0094-114X. DOI: https://doi.org/10.1016/j.mechmachtheory.2021.104429.

[24] C. Ptolemaeus, *System Design, Modeling, and Simulation: Using Ptolemy II*. Berkeley: Ptolemy.org, 2014, ISBN 978-1-304-42106-6.

[25] M. Kielar, O. Handel, and H. Biedermann, "Concurrent hierarchical finite state machines for modeling pedestrian behavioral tendencies", *Transportation Research Part B: Methodological*, vol. 70, pp. 576–584, 2014.

[26] T. Corperation, "Flames makes complex systems analysis simple", 2015, [Online]. Available: http://www.ternion.com/print/FLAMES.pdf.

[27] A. Rajhans, S. Avadhanula, A. Chutinan, *et al.*, "Graphical modeling of hybrid dynamics with simulink and stateflow", in *2018 21st International Conference on Hybrid Systems: Computation and Control (HSCC)*, IEEE, Porto, Portugal, 2018, pp. 247–252.

[28] C. Gomes, C. Thule, D. Broman, P. G. Larsen, and H. Vangheluwe, "Co-simulation: A survey", *ACM Computing Surveys (CSUR)*, vol. 51, no. 3, 2018.

[29] A. M. Uhrmacher, "Dynamic structure in modeling and simulation: A reflective approach", *ACM Transactions on Modeling and Computer Simulation (TOMACS)*, vol. 11, no. 2, pp. 206–232, 2001.

[30] F. J. Barros, "Dynamic structure multiparadigm modeling and simulation", *ACM Transactions on Modeling and Computer Simulation (TOMACS)*, vol. 13, no. 3, pp. 259–275, 2003.

[31] A. Urquia and S. Dormido, "Object-oriented description of hybrid dynamic systems of variable structure", *Simulation: Transactions of the Society for Modeling and Simulation International*, vol. 79, no. 9, pp. 485–493, 2003.

[32] X. Hu, B. P. Zeigler, and S. Mittal, "Variable structure in devs component-based modeling and simulation", *Simulation: Transactions of the Society for Modeling and Simulation International*, vol. 80, no. 2, pp. 91–102, 2005.

[33] P. Fishwick, "Hypermodelling: An integrated approach to dynamic system modelling", *Journal of Simulation*, vol. 6, no. 1, pp. 2–8, 2012.

[34] A. Mehlhase, "A python framework to create and simulate models with variable structure in common simulation environments", *Mathematical and Computer Modelling of Dynamical Systems*, vol. 20, no. 6, pp. 566–583, 2014.

[35] A. Vaswani *et al.*, *Attention is all you need*, 2017. arXiv: 1706.03762.

[36] J. Devlin, M.-W. Chang, K. Lee, and K. Toutanova, *Bert: Pre-training of deep bidirectional transformers for language understanding*, 2019. arXiv: 1810.04805.

[37] T. B. Brown *et al.*, *Language models are few-shot learners*, 2020. arXiv: 2005.14165.

[38] J. Wei *et al.*, *Chain-of-thought prompting elicits reasoning in large language models*, 2023. arXiv: 2201.11903.

[39] H. Liu, C. Li, Q. Wu, and Y. J. Lee, "Visual instruction tuning", in *Advances in Neural Information Processing Systems*, A. Oh *et al.*, Eds., vol. 36, Curran Associates, Inc., 2023, pp. 34 892–34 916.

[40] F. Zhu and J. Tang, "Graphical composite modeling and simulation for multi-aircraft collision avoidance", *Software and Systems Modeling*, 2020.

[41] F. Zhu, Y. Yao, W. Tang, and J. Tang, "A hierarchical composite framework of parallel discrete event simulation for modelling complex adaptive systems", *Simulation Modelling Practice and Theory*, vol. 77, pp. 141–156, 2017.

[42] Q. Dong *et al.*, *A survey on in-context learning*, 2024. arXiv: 2301.00234 [cs.CL].

[43] J. Tang, M. A. Piera, and T. Guasch, "Colored petri net-based traffic collision avoidance system encounter model for the analysis of potential induced collisions", *Transportation Research Part C: Emerging Technologies*, vol. 67, pp. 357–377, 2016.

[44] H. Touvron *et al.*, *Llama: Open and efficient foundation language models*, 2023. arXiv: 2302.13971 [cs.CL].

[45] J. Bai *et al.*, *Qwen-vl: A versatile vision-language model for understanding, localization, text reading, and beyond*, 2023. arXiv: 2308.12966 [cs.CV].

[46] J. Bai *et al.*, *Qwen technical report*, 2023. arXiv: 2309.16609 [cs.CL].

Metasystem for Modeling Emergency Departments

Francisco Mesas*, Manel Taboada*, Dolores Rexachs†, Francisco Epelde‡, Alvaro Wong†, and Emilio Luque†

*Escuelas Universitarias Gimbernat (EUG), Computer Science School, Universitat Autonoma de Barcelona, Sant Cugat del Vallès, Barcelona, Spain
{francisco.mesas,manel.taboada}@eug.es

†Computer Architecture and Operating System Department, Universitat Autonoma de Barcelona, Barcelona, Spain
{dolores.rexachs,emilio.luque,alvaro.wong}@uab.cat

‡Consultant Internal Medicine, University Hospital Parc Tauli, Universitat Autonoma de Barcelona Sabadell, Barcelona, Spain
fepelde@tauli.cat

https://webs.uab.cat/hpc4eas/

***Abstract*—Emergency Departments (EDs) are complex systems that require coordination of medical personnel and resources to manage situations effectively. This research addresses the basic principles for designing a modular system that allows the creation of computational models to improve service quality using available resources. Based on the accumulated knowledge of experts in the ED field, the modular system ensures that each component accurately reflects the particular features present in various health care emergency environments, thus ensuring its adaptability. By applying Agent-Based Modeling and Simulation (ABMS), an analysis of the agents involved, such as patients, doctors, resources and computer systems is considered. ABMS, known for its ability to adapt individually to each agent, allows the design of customized environments that meet the unique needs of various regions and healthcare structures. Inspired by the modularity and versatility of Lego® blocks, this ABMS system seeks to transform a monolithic approach into an adaptable tool that, through a description of the metasystem and an agent box, enables the construction of computational models to potentially improve the quality of emergency care, facilitating strategic decision-making in this critical service.**

Keywords-Emergency Department (ED); Agent-Based Modeling and Simulation (ABMS); Emergency Healthcare Systems; Modular Design; Decision Support Systems (DSS).

I. INTRODUCTION

The Emergency Departments (EDs) currently face an increasingly complex landscape due to saturation experienced in recent years, a phenomenon that highlights both the growing demand for emergency medical care and the need to provide quick and efficient responses in a pressured environment [1].

Simulation stands out as a compelling tool in the context of EDs, allowing us to perform analyses of hypothetical scenarios through "what if" questions [2]. This technique enables anticipation and preparation against potential adverse situations, helping to improve response capacity to the increasing demands that these services may face, especially in critical situations like pandemics or flu outbreaks, which have recently tested their capacity [3]. For instance, through simulation, it is possible to assess the impact that an increase of the patients arrival at ED would have on waiting times and service quality, thus allowing us to devise effective strategies to reduce saturation and ensure adequate care.

In the realm of EDs, simulation techniques are crucial for the analysis of complex processes. Among these, Discrete Event Simulation (DES) and Agent-Based Modeling and Simulation (ABMS) stand out for their effectiveness. DES focuses on the analysis of discrete events over time, allowing evaluation of how each event impacts the flow and operation of the emergency system. It enables us to understand sequences and resource use but might not capture all human interactions. In contrast, ABMS offers a more dynamic and detailed perspective by modeling the behavior and interactions between multiple individual agents, such as patients, doctors, and nurses, as well as their environment. One of the important characteristics of ABMS is the "emergent properties", in other words "the higher-level system properties emerge from the interactions of lower-level subsystems (Agents)" making it the ideal choice according to various studies [4][5].

The variability in the operation of EDs is clearly manifested in the differences in regulatory systems and certifications, e.g., in the field of phlebotomy, we observe a regulatory divergence between the United States and Spain [6]. In the former, certification is a mandatory requirement, while in the latter, it is not required. When considering the implementation of simulation techniques to improve EDs, these structural and regulatory variations must be taken into account. Therefore, it is necessary to adapt simulation solutions to the specific characteristics of each emergency system.

Models and simulators developed up to date by the Research Group of the Universitat Autonoma de Barcelona (UAB) "High Performance Computing For Efficient Applications and Simulation" (HPC4EAS) and other researchers operate in a monolithic manner, which creates certain limitations in terms of adaptability. A monolithic system, by definition, is one in which different components of the software are tightly integrated or unified into a single program developed for an specific case, which can complicate its adaptation to new contexts. Faced with this situation, two initial solutions are presented: modify the existing monolithic model to adapt it to new needs, despite the difficulties this may entail, or develop a new simulator from scratch.

Given the application of the ABMS concept in these systems and inspired by the modularity and versatility of Lego® blocks, a third proposal emerges: to disaggregate those monolithic simulators to create an "agent box." This box would contain all the agents that could be involved in the ED, including medical personnel, patients, administrative staff, and physical resources. This strategy allows the simulator to be fluidly adapted to different ED environments and also to expand the agents and their interactions within the system, a solution that will enable handling the complexity of these environments.

The remainder of this article is structured as follows: Section II provides a concise summary of the previous works by the HPC4EAS group; Section III examines the fundamental properties of the proposed metasystem; Section IV reviews similar research, Section V presents an example of operation, and Section VI describes future plans for the research work.

II. Previous Work

This section presents the results of projects carried out by HPC4EAS, research group from the Department of Computer Architecture and Operating Systems at the Universitat Autònoma de Barcelona (UAB). This project is conducted in collaboration with the staff of the ED at Sabadell Hospital (Corporació Sanitària Parc Taulí), a reference center in the Catalan health system. Additionally, various studies related to the topic are integrated.

The research group has developed both a conceptual model and a computational model (We can consider that the simulator is the implementation of the computational model) that utilizes the ABMS technique, distinguishing between active and passive agents. Active agents are capable of making decisions and acting autonomously, representing individuals, such as doctors, nurses, and patients, who interact and respond to the dynamics of the ED. On the other hand, passive agents do not take initiatives on their own but are essential for executing predetermined processes and enabling interactions, such as hospital information systems, communication networks, and laboratory services. These agents interact within a virtual environment that simulates the areas and processes of an ED, managing different levels of urgency and priority in patient treatment. The interaction between these agents and the modeled environment allows for the replication of the particularities of a real emergency service [7].

The project has evolved through several key phases, starting with the development of a conceptual model derived from a meticulous analysis of the elements of the ED, including the triage system that stratifies urgency into five levels of severity, specifically the Manchester Triage System [8], with level I being the most critical and level V the least. In addition, to mapping other operational aspects and examining the interactions among agents to reproduce the system behavior, the simulator also distributes patients in the ED into two zones, Zone A and Zone B, according to this severity classification, assigning patients with levels I to III to Zone A for priority care, while those with less severity, levels IV and V, are placed in Zone B, designed for less urgent situations. This segmentation is important for managing patient flow [9].

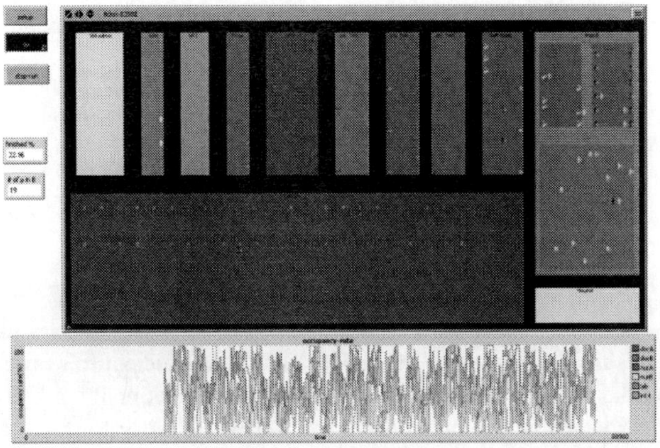

Figure 1. Simulator of the Sabadell Hospital ED, created with NetLogo.

After establishing the conceptual model and understanding the mechanisms of the ED operation, the next step was the creation of the computational model. This model translates the theory and observations of the conceptual model into algorithms and data structures that can be processed by computer systems. In this phase, the behaviors of both active and passive agents are programmed, and the interaction rules and operational procedures, such as the triage system, are encoded. The goal of the computational model is to faithfully reflect the dynamics of a real ED, allowing the simulation of different scenarios and their possible outcomes as can be seen in Figure 1. This model becomes a sophisticated tool for predicting the behavior of the ED at Sabadell Hospital. This scenario was represented using the NetLogo software [10], a modeling environment designed for ABMS, which provides the possibility to accurately design and simulate the operations of a hospital ED.

In the work conducted by various members of the research group, the simulator has been adapted and applied to analyze how to optimally use the limited resources available in the ED [11], to generate information about specific scenarios that, while possible, rarely occur in reality [12], and thus learn about the best way to manage them, or also to analyze, model, and simulate the transmission of the Methicillin-resistant Staphylococcus Aureus (MRSA) virus [13], and its effects on the operation of the ED, in order to explore the potential benefits of adopting preventive measures.

III. General Characteristics of the Metasystem: Lego System

Building on existing work and advancements in the simulation and modeling of EDs using ABMS techniques, we propose the creation of a metasystem, named the Lego® System. This system aims to manage the modularity of ABMS to develop an adaptable simulation environment.

The metasystem will originate from a conceptual model developed with the collaboration of ED specialists and the

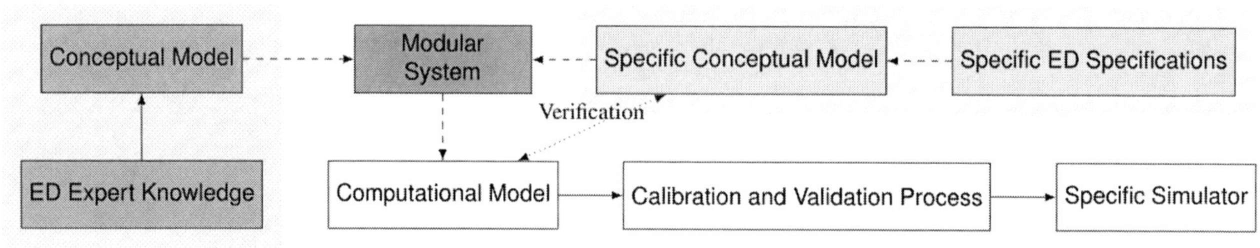

Figure 2. Diagram of the design process of a simulator using a modular system for a specific ED.

disaggregation of current simulators, which will facilitate the definition of standard modules that can be used in various health environments. This will allow for the efficient transition from a specific conceptual design to a computational configuration within the metasystem when it is necessary to develop a computational model for any ED. With the computational model ready, the necessary calibration and validation process must involve the use of specific data that the hospital can offer, and discussions should be held with them to determine the available data to guide this calibration to conclude with a specific simulator. This process is detailed in Figure 2. The section to be analyzed is highlighted in red, while the specific areas of an ED intended to be modeled with the metasystem are highlighted in green.

The goal is to develop a platform that facilitates the creation of computational models of EDs, through an intuitive interface based on "blocks". These blocks represent the various agents and processes involved in the operation of ED and are designed to be customizable. Flexibility is a key point; the system needs to allow for the combination of blocks in multiple ways, thus adapting to the operational particularities of various EDs. For example, it is possible to explore the impact of variations in staff roles, e.g., analyzing the consequences of assigning more or fewer responsibilities to a nurse or simulating scenarios where another team member assumes these tasks. With monolithic systems, such adaptations are costly.

To carry out the disaggregation of these components, it is important to analyze the state variables that will characterize the different agents, as well as define how transitions between these states will occur. In this context, three main categories are established: two corresponding to active agents and one to a passive agent, which will allow us to explore differences in their operation.

Among the active agents, we find common elements that all of them share, such as:

- **Identifier:** Each agent has a unique identifier that allows the system to recognize it in each temporal iteration.
- **Location:** Records the current location of the agent in the ED, which can vary from admission to the treatment area or specific tests.
- **Action:** Agent actions, such as waiting to be called, receiving instructions, or moving between different areas of the ED. These actions will vary by agent.

For the particular case of patients, there are complex state variables and transitions. We can distinguish three specific state variables; personal details, priority level, and communication level. Patients are recognized as one of the most crucial agents in the ED. Their **personal details**, such as age, gender, culture, and religion, are collected and considered to provide tailored treatment. The assignment of a **priority level** based on triage determines the urgency of medical attention, while the **communication level** between the patient and the ED staff is an indicator of the effectiveness of the interaction.

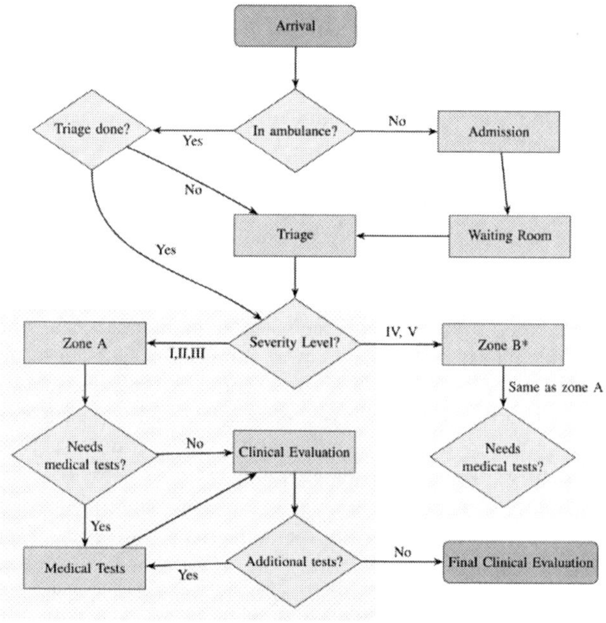

Figure 3. Diagram of the process patients go through in the ED.

The diagram showed in Figure 3 illustrates the process a patient undergoes upon arrival at an ED. It begins with their arrival, a critical point where their unique identifier is assigned, and their initial location or time of arrival is recorded. If they arrive in a medicalized ambulance, triage has already been conducted on-site; otherwise, if they arrive on their own or in a nonmedicalized ambulance, the process starts with their admission.

Priority level assignment occurs during triage, guiding the patient through the system to either to treatment areas, a separated zone (Zone B in the figure) with one specific waiting room and attention boxes for less severe cases (patients with priority level IV or V) or directly to a carebox (Zone A) for patients with more critical conditions (patients with priority level I, II or III).

The level of communication is important at each stage, from assessing whether medical tests are needed to making decisions about additional treatments. An evaluation cycle of treatment and possible re-evaluation continues until a resolution point is reached: the patient is discharged or further measures are taken based on their needs.

Each step of the process reflects the interaction between the patient's state variables and the actions of the ED system.

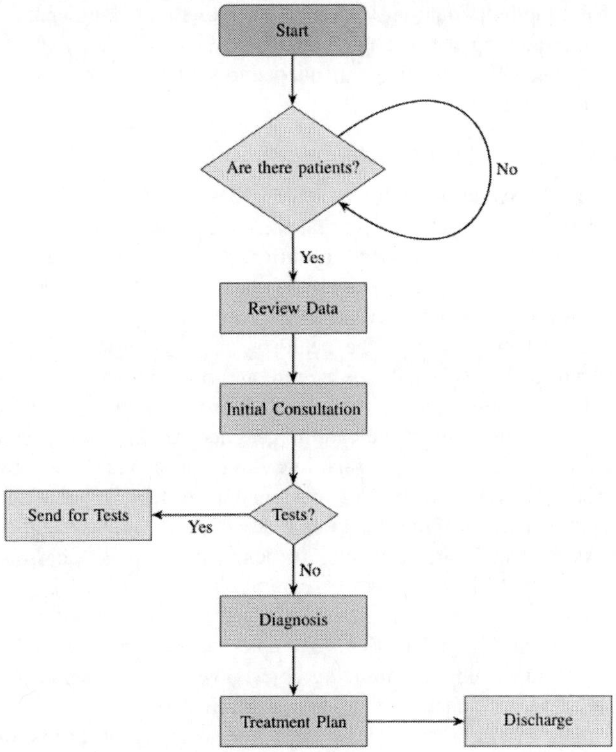

Figure 4. Diagram of the process that doctors undergo in an ED.

Continuing with the exploration of active agents within the ED, doctors are a central figure whose state variables reflect their role in the care environment. Unlike patients, the variables that define a doctor's actions are more straightforward, as they are related to defined tasks and a sequence of clinical steps.

Doctor's actions in the ED range from being inactive, which could mean waiting for the next patient, to more interactive actions, such as asking a patient to come forward, requesting detailed information, making a preliminary diagnosis, and ordering specific tests or treatments. A doctor may also be in an active waiting phase, awaiting the results of tests they have ordered, then making decisions based on those results, such as ordering the patient's discharge from the ED or making a final diagnosis to be entered into the Computer System, as evidenced in Figure 4.

The level of experience of the doctor, classified as low, medium, or high, influences their actions, and is a critical component that impacts the efficiency of work within the ED. A highly experienced doctor may be able to make quicker diagnoses or handle more complex cases in less time. For this reason, the metasystem incorporates a state variable to manage such issues. This is not reflected in the schema because the process remains the same; however, it depends on the state of each agent.

The operation of the Information System (IS) in an ED is essential for efficient and accurate care. It is part of an interactive process where the key decisions that the IS makes are in response to the received requests. Initially, the system checks for pending requests and, based on this, proceeds to obtain reports, register patients, and issue medical alerts. Decisions about whether patient data already exist lead to further actions, such as registering new data or adding them to the existing system. The workflow facilitates the processing of information and the continuous updating of medical records.

As a passive agent, the IS depends on interactions with active agents, such as the medical or administrative staff of the ED, to change state. The system's propensity for errors is classified into low, medium, and high levels, which can affect the operability of the ED.

The IS, as a passive agent within the ED, plays a significant role in coordinating between the different components of the healthcare system. The ability to process and issue information accurately is necessary to maintain a smooth workflow and to ensure that patients receive the necessary care at the appropriate time. It is a component that supports all the operations of the ED, from admission and triage to the patient being discharged.

The interaction between doctors and patients, mediated by the information system, is a delicate dance of consultations, diagnostics, and decisions that advance the patient through the care process, as reflected in the discussed figures.

IV. RELATED WORK

The adaptability of simulation models to various health systems seeks to improve EDs. This flexibility will allow the implementation of the proposed modular metasystem, which can be adjusted to the specifics of different emergency care environments.

There are initiatives by research groups that have used simulation to enhance the effectiveness of EDs. The 3S Research Group and the Shelford team in England have conducted simulations at the University Hospital of Dublin [14] and in specific cases of the ED in London [15] respectively, offering valuable reference models for our proposal.

Moreover, it is important to analyze health systems in their social and economic context, as factors such as funding and access to health services, vary significantly between countries [16].

TABLE I. COMPARISON OF HEALTHCARE MODELS

Model	Funding	Control and Management	Coverage and Features
Beveridge	Income taxes	Government	Universal, public
Bismarck	Social insurance	State regulates	Employment-dependent, copayments
National Insurance	Taxes and insurances	Mixed	Universal, greater choice of providers
Out-of-Pocket	Private	Individual	Limited access, no financial protection

Analyzing how health systems function provides a more global perspective. It's necessary to evaluate the different health models found in each country. According to the World Health Organization, there are four main models [17]. Each has its distinctive characteristics regarding funding, management, and coverage.

The Beveridge model, implemented in countries like Spain, Portugal, and Finland, is characterized by its funding through income taxes, with the government assuming total control of healthcare management and providing universal coverage. This approach contrasts with the Bismarck model, prevalent in Austria, Germany, and Switzerland, where funding comes from mandatory contributions to social insurance funds. Although the state regulates healthcare entities, coverage depends on the individual's employment status, and copayments are included for certain services.

On the other hand, the National Health Insurance Model, found in Japan, Canada, and South Korea, combines elements of both previous models offering universal and equitable coverage, regardless of employment affiliation [18]. This model allows a greater choice of healthcare providers. Lastly, the Out-of-Pocket model is distinguished by the absence of collective funding, leaving individuals to face healthcare costs without a financial safety net, which limits universal access to health.

Each model reflects a different philosophy regarding the role of government, individual responsibility, and the principles of social solidarity. While the Beveridge and National Health Insurance models focus on universal coverage guaranteed by the state, the Bismarck and Out-of-Pocket models present a more segmented or individualized approach to healthcare coverage, which causes different types of ED operations in each case. These differences are reflected in Table I.

These factors can lead to different roles and internal functioning aimed at optimizing available resources. For example, the approach to phlebotomy in the United States, where there is specific training for this skill, differs from other countries with different training approaches, such as in Spain, where nurses are responsible for this process. With the new modular "Lego®" system, the need to adapt the simulator to these variations is no longer a problem, as the modules can be customized and reconfigured to reflect any health system.

There are tools seeking something similar like VisualizER, a DES tool that exemplifies how simulation can be applied to optimize EDs [19]. Although it allows effective simulation of emergency operations, it does not offer the capability to model the individual behavior of agents, which is a crucial component for anticipating unforeseen events.

Our proposal for an ABMS-based metasystem advances beyond existing DES solutions by leveraging the advantages of ABMS for creating modules that allow the result to emerge from the individual interaction of agents. This feature enables understanding and managing the often unpredictable dynamics of EDs, thus providing an adaptable system for healthcare professionals.

V. OPERATION OF THE METASYSTEM

In the metasystem for modeling EDs, it is crucial to have an interface or set of tools that facilitate customization of the system to the specific needs of different hospital environments. This functionality allows users to manipulate and redefine the stages and agents involved in the process easily.

Each component of the health system, represented by an agent, can be selected, configured, and placed within a workflow. The proposal is to drag and drop components, thus modeling the flow of the care process according to the criteria of each ED. Through this interface, for example, a new triage procedure specifically designed to respond to pandemic emergencies could be integrated, adjusting the metasystem to reflect changes in protocols. To achieve this, it is necessary to establish a basic form of communication between agents through primitives that are easily interchangeable among them and capable of adaptation. Examples of such primitives include conversing and utilizing objects, which are essential for defining each agent's own internal mechanism.

There will always be a need for a series of forms or commands that allow specifying and modifying the properties and behaviors of each agent. This functionality is relevant when wanting to add a new agent, e.g., a 'pandemic triage agent.' Here, the person in charge has the opportunity to access a library of predefined agents and select the one that fits their needs. Subsequently, the functions of this agent can be customized by adjusting parameters and behaviors.

In the event that a necessary agent is not predefined, tools are provided for users to create one from scratch. This allows the system to be adaptable, enabling each healthcare center the ability to mold the metasystem to their operational reality.

Figure 5 shows the structure of an ED. At the bottom, the set of "agent box" can be observed, a collection of roles and functions from which one can choose to assign to the different phases of the care process. For example, during the admission phase, a distinction is made between a process for a public ED and a private one. In the triage phase, a nurse specialized

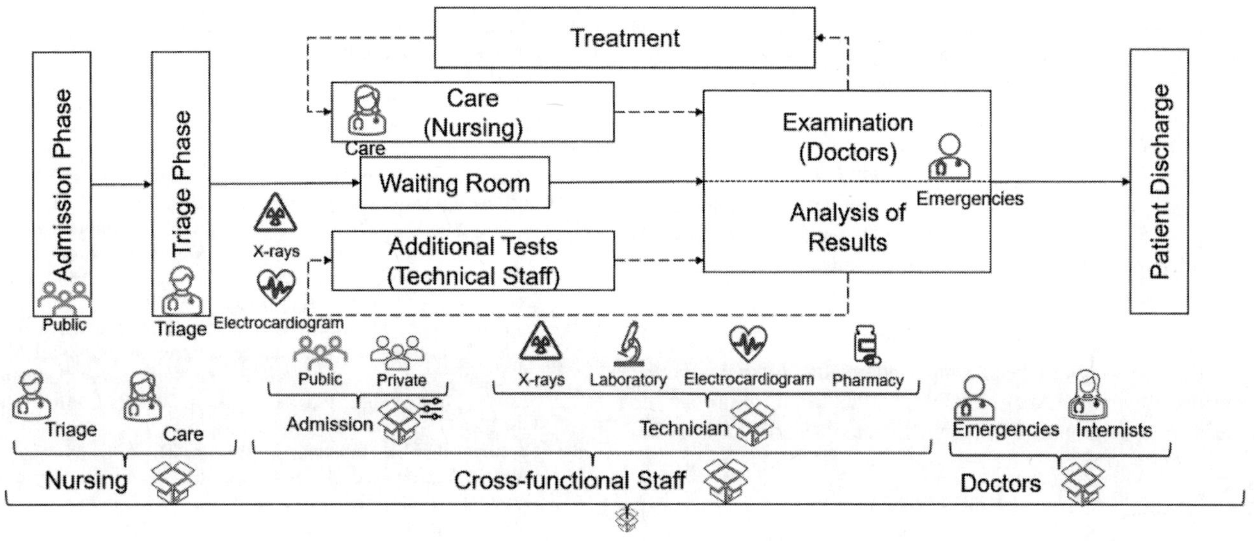

Figure 5. Example of Modules Utilized in a ED.

in this task is required. However, if the situation demands the incorporation of a triage nurse with greater experience due to an increase in the complexity of cases or the need to expedite the process, this new type of professional could be added. This process would be carried out by duplicating the configuration of the existing triage nurse and adjusting her parameters of behavior and performance according to the additional experience she brings to the process.

Consider the scenario where an ED in Spain is public, in such a case, this specific setting can be selected to work within the system. Similarly, settings for other stages, such as Triage, Waiting Room, and Performing Additional Tests can be customized to specify the capabilities and processes for each element of the system. This customization process allows the system to transition smoothly from the general agent-based configuration shown with the box to a more specific configuration that can be shown with the selected agent boxes in the diagram of the Figure 5.

This tailored approach ensures that each component of the ED could operates optimally according to the defined roles and requirements, enhancing both efficiency and patient care.

VI. Conclusion and Future Work

Simulation in EDs is greatly beneficial in addressing the increasing complexity and saturation these services currently experience. The ability to analyze problematic situations in advance through the simulation of hypothetical scenarios allows EDs to prepare and respond effectively to adverse situations, especially in critical contexts, such as pandemics or disease outbreaks. Simulation not only improves response capacity to growing demand but also contributes to the strategic planning of EDs.

ABMS stands out as the appropriate tool for simulating EDs, surpassing DES in terms of the ability to model the complexities of such systems. ABMS, with its "emergent properties", allows for a detailed representation of interactions among multiple agents, such as patients, doctors, and nurses, and their environment, capturing the essence of human processes.

The development of simulators using ABMS represents a significant advance, allowing models to be adapted to different EDs. The transition from monolithic models to a LEGO-type modular system, referred to as an "agent box," facilitates the adaptation and expansion of simulators to meet various configurations and needs of ED. This modularity allows for efficient customization and reconfiguration, reflecting any health system and its operational particularities.

This simulation proposal differs from other solutions, such as DES and tools like VisualizER, in its focus on agent adaptation and modeling. Through the "emergent properties" of ABMS, it is possible to model individual behavior and interactions between agents, a crucial component for managing the often unpredictable dynamics of EDs. This provides an adaptable system for healthcare professionals, enabling more effective management of EDs.

However, there are limitations and potential future directions for the expansion of this technology. One is the number of predefined modules in the "agent box," which could be addressed by creating a common repository where modules adapted to new needs and contexts are shared and updated. Moreover, expanding the use of modular systems in EDs to other healthcare and geographic contexts could provide valuable insights and enhance the efficiency of EDs globally.

In conclusion, the proposal of an ABMS-based metasystem for the simulation of EDs contributes to a better understanding and management of these services. Through the ability to model the complexity of human interactions, this technology opens new possibilities for preparing EDs for current and future challenges. The evolution towards modular systems and collaboration in the development of modules can further enhance simulation capabilities, offering continuous improvement of EDs.

In the future, the Delphi method, a process used to arrive at a group opinion or decision by surveying a panel of experts [20], will be necessary to build a comprehensive conceptual model and develop the meta-model. This analysis will involve multidisciplinary collaboration with clinical expertise and the use of ABMS.

ACKNOWLEDGMENTS

This research has been supported by the Agencia Estatal de Investigación (AEI), Spain and the Fondo Europeo de Desarrollo Regional (FEDER) UE, under contract PID2020-112496GB-I00.

REFERENCES

[1] M. Samadbeik *et al.*, "Patient flow in emergency departments: A comprehensive umbrella review of solutions and challenges across the health system," *BMC Health Services Research*, vol. 24, no. 1, p. 274, 2024, ISSN: 1472-6963. DOI: 10.1186/s12913-024-10725-6.

[2] F. McGuire, "Using simulation to reduce length of stay in emergency departments," in *Proceedings of Winter Simulation Conference*, 1994, pp. 861–867. DOI: 10.1109/WSC.1994.717446.

[3] M. E. Reschen *et al.*, "Impact of the covid-19 pandemic on emergency department attendances and acute medical admissions," *BMC Emergency Medicine*, vol. 21, no. 1, p. 143, 2021. DOI: 10.1186/s12873-021-00529-w.

[4] T. Monks *et al.*, "Strengthening the reporting of empirical simulation studies: Introducing the stress guidelines," *Journal of Simulation*, vol. 13, no. 1, pp. 55–67, 2019. DOI: 10.1080/17477778.2018.1442155.

[5] M. Yousefi, M. Yousefi, and F. S. Fogliatto, "Simulation-based optimization methods applied in hospital emergency departments: A systematic review," *SIMULATION*, vol. 96, no. 10, pp. 791–806, 2020. DOI: 10.1177/0037549720944483.

[6] Piazza *et al.*, "It's Not Just a Needlestick: Exploring Phlebotomists' Knowledge, Training, and Use of Comfort Measures in Pediatric Care to Improve the Patient Experience," *The Journal of Applied Laboratory Medicine*, vol. 3, no. 5, pp. 847–856, Mar. 2019, ISSN: 2576-9456. DOI: 10.1373/jalm.2018.027573.

[7] M. Taboada, E. Cabrera, F. Epelde, M. L. Iglesias, and E. Luque, "Agent-based emergency decision-making aid for hospital emergency departments," *Emergencias*, vol. 24, pp. 189–195, 2012.

[8] J. M. Zachariasse *et al.*, "Validity of the manchester triage system in emergency care: A prospective observational study," *PloS one*, vol. 12, no. 2, e0170811, 2017. DOI: 10.1371/journal.pone.0170811.

[9] L. Zhengchun, D. Rexachs, F. Epelde, and E. Luque, "A simulation and optimization based method for calibrating agent-based emergency department models under data scarcity," *Computers and Industrial Engineering*, vol. 103, pp. 300–309, 2017. DOI: 10.1016/j.cie.2016.11.036.

[10] Center for Connected Learning and Computer-Based Modeling, Northwestern University, *Netlogo*, https://ccl.northwestern.edu/netlogo/, Retrieved: July, 2024.

[11] E. Cabrera, M. Taboada, M. L. Iglesias, F. Epelde, and E. Luque, "Optimization of healthcare emergency departments by agent-based simulation," *Procedia CS*, vol. 4, pp. 1880–1889, Dec. 2011. DOI: 10.1016/j.procs.2011.04.204.

[12] E. Bruballa, M. Taboada, E. Cabrera, D. Rexachs, and E. Luque, "Simulation of unusual or extreme situations of hospital emergency departments," in *ICCS Procedia Computer Science*, Nice, France: IARIA, 2014, pp. 209–212, ISBN: 978-1-61208-371-1.

[13] C. Jaramillo, M. Taboada, F. Epelde, D. Rexachs, and E. Luque, "Agent based model and simulation of mrsa transmission in emergency departments," *Procedia Computer Science*, vol. 51, pp. 443–452, 2015, International Conference On Computational Science, ICCS 2015, ISSN: 1877-0509. DOI: https://doi.org/10.1016/j.procs.2015.05.267.

[14] W. Abo-Hamad and A. Arisha, "Simulation-based framework to improve patient experience in an emergency department," *European Journal of Operational Research*, vol. 224, no. 1, pp. 154–166, 2013, ISSN: 0377-2217. DOI: https://doi.org/10.1016/j.ejor.2012.07.028.

[15] T. Godfrey *et al.*, "Supporting emergency department risk mitigation with a modular and reusable agent-based simulation infrastructure," in *2023 Winter Simulation Conference (WSC)*, IEEE, 2023, pp. 162–173. DOI: 10.1109/WSC60868.2023.10407894.

[16] O. O. Oleribe *et al.*, "Identifying key challenges facing healthcare systems in africa and potential solutions," eng, *International journal of general medicine*, vol. 12, pp. 395–403, 2019. DOI: 10.2147/IJGM.S223882.

[17] H. K. Mitonga and A. P. K. Shilunga, "International health care systems: Models, components, and goals," in *Handbook of Global Health*. Cham: Springer International Publishing, 2020, pp. 1–20. DOI: 10.1007/978-3-030-05325-3_60-1.

[18] C. Cuadrado, F. Crispi, M. Libuy, G. Marchildon, and C. Cid, "National health insurance: A conceptual framework from conflicting typologies," *Health Policy*, vol. 123, no. 7, pp. 621–629, Jul. 2019, Epub 2019 May 18, ISSN: 1872-6054. DOI: 10.1016/j.healthpol.2019.05.013.

[19] ER-Visualizer, *Visualizer: Emergency room visualization tool*, https://github.com/ER-Visualizer/Visualizer, Retrieved: July, 2024.

[20] J. de Meyrick, "The delphi method and health research," *Health Education*, vol. 103, no. 1, pp. 7–16, Feb. 2003, ISSN: 0965-4283. DOI: 10.1108/09654280310459112.

Agent-Based Modeling of Urban Traffic Scenarios for Improved Priority Vehicle Mobility

Toni Gonzalez-Cuevas Álvaro Wong Remo Suppi
Department of Computer Architecture and Operating Systems
Universitat Autònoma de Barcelona
Barcelona, Spain
e-mail: {antonio.gonzalezc | alvaro.wong | remo.suppi}@uab.cat

***Abstract*—This study is oriented to analyzing urban mobility challenges, with a focus on improving traffic flow conditions for priority vehicles in complex urban environments. Leveraging Agent-Based Models (ABM) in conjunction with Geographic Information Systems (GIS), the research aims to simulate various traffic scenarios to enhance the efficiency of urban mobility, with a particular emphasis on the movement of priority vehicles. The investigation explores the crucial role of priority vehicles, including but not limited to ambulances, within urban settings. It examines factors such as traffic congestion, infrastructure design, and the impact of traffic management strategies on the mobility of these essential services. A key component of this research involves conducting "What if?" analyses under different traffic conditions, such as mixed traffic flows, dedicated lanes, and emergency route prioritization. These simulations aim to evaluate the potential outcomes of various urban planning strategies on the efficiency of priority vehicle movement and overall traffic flow dynamics. This implementation serves as a foundational step towards understanding and simulating urban traffic scenarios. In the future, the project will integrate priority vehicles into the model and move to a High Performance Computing (HPC) environment. This article outlines the current state of the traffic model, focusing on the NetLogo implementation, and previews the upcoming integration of priority vehicles and the transition to HPC. While initially centered around Barcelona, the methodologies developed through this study are designed to be adaptable for application in other urban areas. The ultimate goal is to contribute to the development of effective traffic management strategies that prioritize the mobility of priority vehicles, thereby enhancing public safety and operational efficiency across densely populated urban environments.**

Keywords-Agent Based Modeling; traffic simulation; urban mobility simulation; real-world data; priority vehicles.

I. INTRODUCTION

Urban traffic management is a key focus in city planning. It covers a wide range of topics, including transportation planning, traffic control, and intelligent transportation systems. It also addresses congestion management, public transit, road safety, special event coordination, sustainability, and the use of data and analytics. Effective traffic management is crucial for ensuring efficient, secure, and sustainable mobility within urban areas and across broader transport networks.

Within the urban landscape, the occurrence of emergency situations demands a specialized approach to traffic management. It is essential to facilitate the rapid and safe navigation of emergency response vehicles—such as ambulances, fire trucks, and police cars—from their bases to the scene of an emergency. This necessitates the strategic planning of routes that not only minimize travel times but also prioritize safety and efficiency throughout the journey [1]. Particularly in the case of ambulances, route planning acquires added significance, covering both the journey to the emergency site and the subsequent transport of patients to medical facilities. Determining optimal routes under these conditions is vital, highlighting the necessity for flexible planning and management strategies that can adapt to various emergency situations.

Recent developments in emergency management, specifically regarding ambulances, have introduced a variety of approaches aimed at improving response times and maximizing coverage [2]. These innovations span from optimizing ambulance locations and creating platforms that combine route optimization with real-time patient monitoring to adopting Internet of Things (IoT)-based solutions. Furthermore, considerations extend beyond mere arrival times to include selecting safe routes that circumvent accident-prone areas, traffic lights, and adverse environmental conditions. There are also instances where the nearest hospital may lack the required capabilities to treat a patient, adding another layer of complexity to routing decisions.

The management of priority vehicles poses a complex challenge, involving aspects such as identifying alternative routes, collaborating with local authorities, signaling emergency routes, communicating with citizens, monitoring in real-time, ensuring adaptability and flexibility, coordinating with emergency services, training staff, evaluating infrastructure capabilities, and integrating technology. Effective planning of emergency routes is critical for guaranteeing quick and safe responses within complex systems, thereby aiding efficient traffic management during critical moments.

This ongoing research aims to address emergency situations through agent-based simulation, utilizing real-world data to analyze mobility flows and interactions among various vehicle types [3], as well as the conditions and outcomes of these interactions. By incorporating Geographic Information Systems (GIS) to tailor the simulation environment, the study aspires to create open simulations that are applicable beyond specific cities. The combination of Agent-Based Modeling (ABM), GIS environments, and real-world data will enable the analysis of different scenarios and strategies within urban or complex mobility environments, allowing for the examination of various episodes and strategies, whether real or hypothetical.

As this research progresses, the next steps will focus on the calibration and validation of the simulation model, enhancing its ability to integrate priority vehicles and generate different types of scenario simulations. This will pave the way for more accurate and insightful analyses of urban traffic management and emergency response strategies.

The next section of this article will explore the current state of the art, focusing on existing solutions and their applications. Section 3 will detail the simulation infrastructure and environment, including the architecture, implementation of the vehicle model, data acquisition methods, GIS system integration, and preliminary simulation results related to a roadway in Barcelona. Finally, Section 4 will present conclusions drawn from the findings thus far and outline future directions for research and development.

II. Related work | Methods

As urban traffic management evolves, the demand for accurate traffic simulations is increasing. In 2022, the market for traffic simulation systems was valued at around USD 4.10 billion. It is projected to grow significantly, reaching USD 7.83 trillion by 2030 [4]. Among the various approaches to traffic simulation, microscopic simulation stands out, holding a 40.97% market share in 2022 [4]. These models are increasingly essential for testing connected and automated driving technologies under real-world conditions, providing transportation managers and engineers with critical tools for improving traffic flow and reducing congestion globally.

Geographically, North America leads the global transportation simulation and predictive analytics market, largely due to its advanced infrastructure and early adoption of technology in the transportation sector. Europe follows closely, driven by the EU's emphasis on sustainable transport and smart cities initiatives, as well as emissions restrictions and traffic management regulations that encourage the adoption of predictive analytics and simulation tools [5].

A variety of traffic simulation software supports different simulation approaches. For microscopic simulations, notable examples include A/B Testing, Paramics Discovery, MATSim OS, OpenTrafficSim, CityFlow, VSim RTI, SIDRA, and Micromac. Macroscopic analyses are facilitated by software such as PTV Balance & Epics, Cube Voyager, and Quadstone Paramics Discovery, while mesoscopic approaches utilize software like TransModeler, Aimsun Next, AnyLogic, and SimWalk. Commercial offerings such as PTV Visum for macroscopic analysis, INRO for microscopic and mesoscopic levels, and open-source solutions like Eclipse SUMO and MATSim are also highlighted. Additionally, NetLogo, Repast, and MASON cater to broader simulation needs, including urban traffic simulation [6][7].

Strategies for traffic control, particularly concerning priority vehicles, focus on minimizing response times. These strategies encompass route optimization, traffic signal prioritization, and lane reservation. However, employing a single strategy is insufficient, underscoring the importance of integrating multiple solutions for a robust outcome [8]. Efforts towards optimization aim to reduce total response times, with implementations varying from genetic algorithms to Dijkstra algorithm applications integrated with GIS [1][5][9][10].

Agent-Based Modeling presents a unique opportunity to model complex urban systems, capturing human behavior and its evolution over space and time. Despite its advantages, challenges remain in calibration and validation due to computational demands and the complexity of evaluating interactions across multiple scales within ABM models. Moreover, the integration of real-world data and, more specifically, real-time data into ABM is an emerging field, with dynamic recalibration and state updates posing significant hurdles [11][12]. As this research progresses, future steps will address these challenges by focusing on the calibration and validation of the simulation model. Enhancing the model's ability to integrate priority vehicles and generate varied scenario simulations will be pivotal. These advancements will enable more accurate and insightful analyses of urban traffic dynamics and emergency response strategies, contributing to the ongoing development of effective traffic management solutions.

III. Simulation infrastructure & environment representation

The primary goal of this research is to develop and validate urban mobility maps using agent-based simulation models. This includes integrating GIS-based infrastructure models that handle both mixed and priority traffic. We aim to ensure robust validation with real-world data, focus on decision support systems (DSS), and design an agent-based model that can transition to High Performance Computing (HPC) environments for enhanced performance.

The study goes beyond traditional analyzes by taking an approach to obtaining answers to questions such as: "What if?" (What if we have one less lane on the road? What if we have a part of the road not operational and traffic must be diverted to other roads? What if a bus lane replaces a lane of the road, limiting traffic?, etc.) covering a spectrum of factors, including mixed traffic dynamics, the introduction of dedicated cycle lanes and the reduction of lanes for private vehicles. In particular, we expanded our approach to prioritizing routes for emergency vehicles, recognizing the critical role they play in urban safety and response times.

The marked layout seeks to use traffic control strategies related to priority vehicles, such as different techniques for lane reservation, route optimization and signal prioritization. Regarding the typology of existing priority vehicles, ambulances are of special interest due to their relevance in the route to the point of emergency as well as the route to take the injured to the hospital. In addition to the time needed to reach the incident, factors such as guaranteeing a safe route to the destination hospital (the closest hospital may not be the appropriate one), and the time at which the incident occurred, among others, are elements to highlight.

A. Architecture

The proposal aims to extract geographical areas for analysis using limiting coordinates and bounding boxes based on GIS. From these areas, it will extract various environmental layers such as terrain, rivers, roads, and buildings. These layers and their characteristics will then form the foundation for the model's representation. On this basis, the different types of agents are generated and distributed, representing the elements of the simulation and forming the global set, environment and agents, for the simulation.

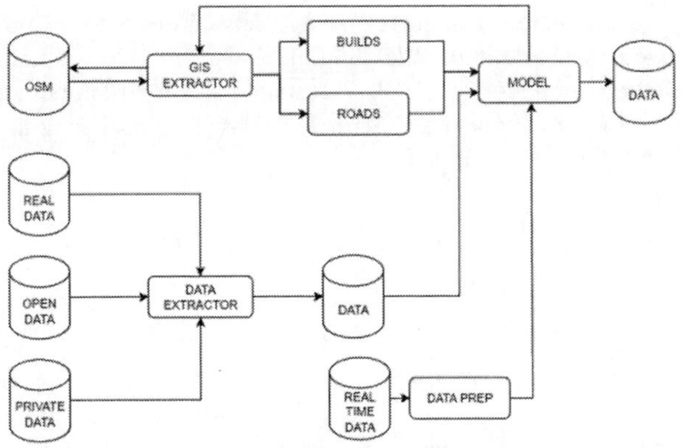

Figure 1. Block diagram for data ingestion.

The architecture of our proposal is illustrated in Figure 1. The model has as inputs, on the one hand, the elements that form the environment that, as shown, is now worked with buildings and roads. These elements of the environment are obtained from Open Street Maps (OSM) [13], using the GIS extraction block. In addition to the environment data, the model receives static data inputs from different Open Data sources, real data that can be available, and private data sources that can be accessed. This static information is complemented with real-time information that allows the model to adjust with data from direct sources of information. Using the environment information, along with the static and dynamic data provided to the model, we can configure and develop the simulation scenarios. Once the scenarios are prepared, we can proceed to execute the simulation. This will generate the results that will allow the evaluation of the effectiveness of the different configurations made on the agents' environment.

B. Vehicle model implementation

The model used for vehicles has a series of characteristics that allow its configuration where we have, as direct inputs (see Figure 2):

- Acceleration
- Deceleration
- Limit speed
- Probability of turning when reaching intersection
- "Patience" level
- Maximum speed
- Minimum speed
- Number of passengers
- Priority
- Type of vehicle

Acceleration and deceleration are key variables for analyzing traffic flow. They determine the speed limits that the model uses to assign different speeds to vehicles, always adhering to the established speed limit. The turning probability will be used to decide whether a vehicle will change lanes at an intersection or continue on its current path. The patience level is used for cases in which faster vehicles catch up with slower ones and have to reduce their speed, where they consume their patience level, reaching, in certain cases, exhausting it and, as a consequence, making a lane change on the road. The maximum and minimum speeds are calculated taking the limit speed as a reference. The type of vehicle and the number of passengers also influence the way a vehicle travels on the road. Finally, priority defines how vehicles will react in the way. Furthermore, for the execution of each simulation it is necessary to indicate the GIS coordinates that allow delimiting the work area and extracting the characteristics of the environment and the number of vehicles that determines the volume of mobile agents that will be in the simulation.

The environment model represents how static elements will influence traffic flow. Elements such as signals, traffic lights or pedestrian crossings that are elements that can regulate and coordinate the flow of traffic, minimize conflicts and reduce congestion.

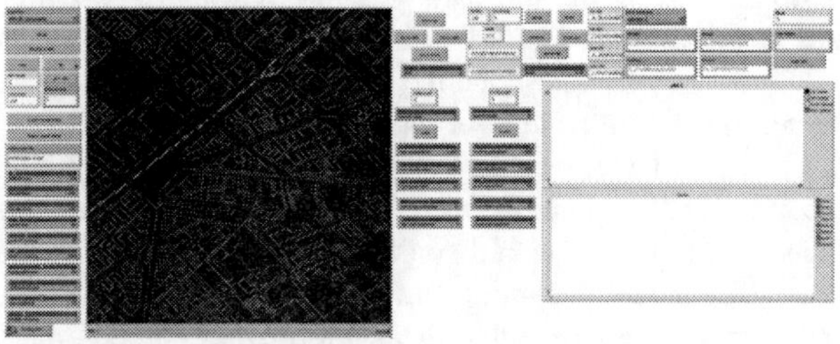

Figure 2. A screenshot showing the interface of the model using the NetLogo platform

The methodology chosen for this work is a phased incremental development strategy, structured around four main tasks:

1) Use data collected and extracted from the real world
2) Integrate GIS data into agent-based simulation environments
3) Develop mobility models based on real data within the GIS infrastructure
4) Formulate multi-lane traffic models, with a specific focus on an urban road characterized by high-density controlled traffic and its immediate surroundings.

Each aspect of the methodology has been developed to facilitate data collection from the real world. Software has been created to recognize various types of vehicles, working directly with videos captured on-site. This software analyzes the footage to extract data on vehicle type, lane occupancy, direction, speed, and distance. The initial version has been based on an improved version of DeepSORT and YOLOv5 libraries [14] to gather information from the most representative streets in Barcelona, analyzing various traffic types. This approach allowed us to obtain speed distributions and measure the distances between vehicles.

Integrating geographic data into an agent-based simulation environment enables us to visualize the roads used in the simulation. It also allows us to incorporate environmental data into the model. NetLogo [15] has be ssen selected as the simulation environment, which supports GIS extensions. NetLogo has been selected because it is designed for agent-based modeling solutions, without limiting access to its functions and features, flexibility, cost and research focus. Customization and modification to specific needs may not be possible with proprietary software due to restrictions on source code access. This development has been designed as a first functional simulation infrastructure in order to verify the main concepts and transfer it to HPC infrastructure (based on Repast [16]) for large simulations. Figure 3, on the left, shows the simulation environment with the representation of the environment in white and the traffic routes, active elements in the simulation, in blue. Currently, the road characteristics includes various data points, name, geographic coordinates (longitude and latitude), direction, angle, road type, number of lanes, maximum speed, and interconnection points with other roads, among others.

The right side of Figure 3 shows a screenshot of the analysis area acquired directly from the Open Street Maps [13]. Comparing the left part with the right part of Figure 3 and taking into account that the analysis environment reflects only the road of interest and the existing buildings, we can see the accuracy and veracity of the data represented.

The development of the model integrates the information, presented above, about the roads in the GIS representation (see Figure 3) and works directly on this rich representation in NetLogo. The model integrates data on each road's characteristics and sections. This provides direct information on coordinates, distances between points, and angles of road elements. It also includes details such as road type, number of lanes, maximum speed, road name, and whether it is paved. These attributes are available to each agent during the simulation. Regarding the agents, they have been implemented with the variables reflected above where we can see their representation in Figure 3.

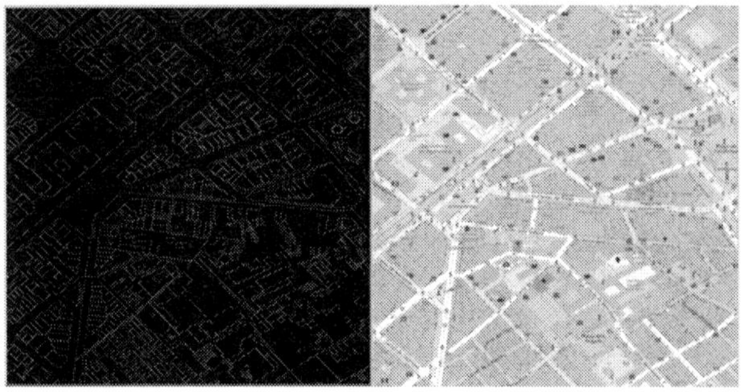

Figure 3. Analysis area.

The current model already represents a multilane system, of a specific high-density road in Barcelona, Gran Via de les Corts Catalanes, as well as its surroundings, representing the different options through the data obtained through GIS and the adjustment of the available parameters.

C. Data acquisition

As mentioned earlier, initially, we characterized Barcelona's street traffic by capturing its key features through video recordings. Using AI libraries, we detected vehicles and their attributes to model typical traffic flow. Additionally, we integrated GIS data into a NetLogo-based model created from this real-world data.

To calculate the angular distance between two points on a sphere using latitude and longitude, we use the Haversine method (equation 1) [17]. Haversine is very popular and frequently used when a GIS implementation or analyzing path and fields are developed:

$$\begin{aligned} a &= sin^2(\Delta\varphi/2) + cos\varphi_1 * cos\varphi_2 * sin^2(\Delta\lambda/2) \\ c &= 2 * atan2(\sqrt{a}, \sqrt{(1-a)}) \\ d &= R * c \end{aligned} \quad (1)$$

In the Haversine equation where φ is latitude, λ is longitude, R is earth's radius (mean radius = 6,371km) is how we translate the above formula to include latitude and longitude coordinates. $\Delta\varphi$ is the difference in latitude and $\Delta\lambda$ is the difference in longitude.

To obtain the direction of the vehicle, its angle, aligned with the direction of the road, the formula shown is used [18]:

$$\begin{aligned} \theta = atan2(sin\Delta\varphi * cos\varphi_2, cos\varphi_1 * sin\varphi_2 \\ - sin\varphi_1 * cos\varphi_2 * cos\Delta\varphi) \end{aligned} \quad (2)$$

where φ_1,λ_1 is the start point, φ_2,λ_2 the end point ($\Delta\lambda$ is the difference in longitude). The Haversine Formula is used to calculate distances during the initial setup phase. This step involves importing all relevant data for the map area into NetLogo. All tasks are performed within the NetLogo graphical environment. If it's the first time working with the map, the global work area is used to execute all data generation steps. This process extracts all environmental characteristics from the global map, including the sequences of geographical points defining each road. It also involves calculating distances between points and angles of each road segment using the Haversine formula.

This information will be readily available during the simulation, allowing agents to access it without additional calculations. This setup enables us to concentrate on managing agents and their interactions. During the simulation, agents will calculate distances and direction angles as they move along the roads, based on their defined behavior.

D. GIS integration

At this point the solution has been evolved, enriching the information about the roads in the GIS representation and a model has been implemented that already works directly on this enriched representation in NetLogo. The current model integrates detailed road characteristics, including coordinates, distances between points, and angles of road elements. It also provides information on road type, number of lanes, maximum speed, road name, and paving status. Additionally, it includes links between routes and their connection points. This comprehensive integration has enabled the model to evolve into a multilane representation.

Figure 4. Simulation screenshot showing cars on different lanes.

Figure 4 illustrates the partial simulation area, showcasing the vehicles in various colors. The colors of each vehicle represent the lane in which they are located. For example, the yellow color represents the vehicles that are in lane 1, the leftmost one, the cyan color represents the vehicles that are in lane 2 of the road, and so on. This allows us to visually identify the vehicles on each lane and define how the vehicles behave when they are on the different lanes and the interaction between them when they move along the different lanes.

Based on the field analysis data -covering vehicle types, lane occupancy, direction, speed, distance, and their evolution over time- the validation criteria for the simulation results have been established.

Currently, the simulation provides information on the evolution of maximum, average, and minimum speeds, as well as the overall vehicle volume at each moment (see Figure 5). In addition to the speeds, the simulation provides us with information about the existing speeds in the different lanes and how they vary over time. In addition to speed lane data, the simulation also offers insights into the variations in speeds across different lanes and how these change over time. In the case of speeds, the results show how global speeds evolve (see Figure 5), where maximum speeds between 46.1 km/h and 63.9 km/h and minimum speeds of 12.2 km/h have been obtained due to congestion, and 34 km/h as the most stable value. The average speeds have been maintained between 32.6 km/h and 47.6 km/h for a volume of 20 vehicles on the road.

The analysis of the lanes, depicted in Figure 6, reveals that the fourth lane from the left (colored yellow) among the five lanes has the highest maximum speed. It also shows the second lowest minimum speed of 14 km/h, while the lowest minimum speed is 12 km/h, observed in the first lane (colored gray). Overall, the average speeds across sections range between 22 km/h and 47 km/h.

The conclusions drawn from the results reaffirm previous findings, which validated that traffic fluidity primarily depends on traffic intensity, and that acceleration and deceleration directly influence traffic flow. The next phase of our research focuses on improving the imported road characteristics, integrating them into the model, and incorporating traffic signals and various types of vehicles.

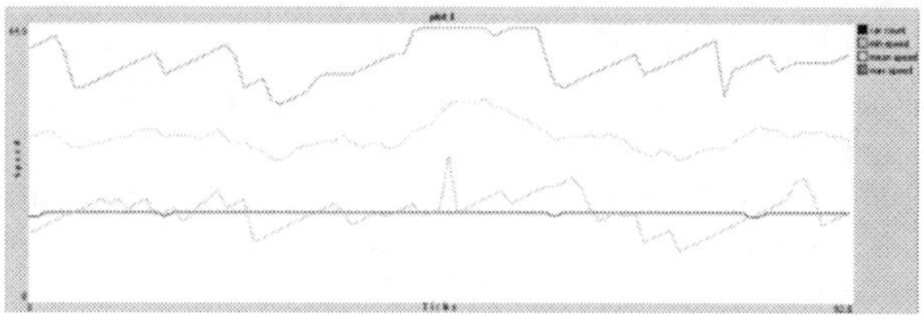

Figure 5. Simulation screenshot showing the number and speed of vehicles.

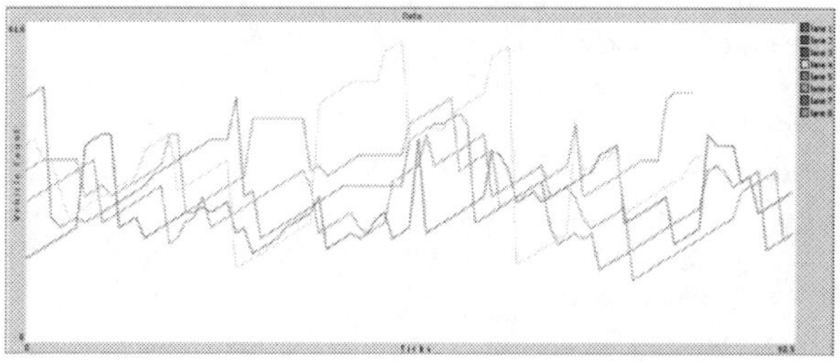

Figure 6. Simulation screenshot showing lane occupancy level.

Currently, the model integrates vehicles based on the characteristics of the represented roads. The approach will evolve to enhance both the environmental model and the vehicle types representation. Next, priority vehicles will be incorporated using techniques discussed earlier, such as implementing priority signals, reserving lanes, and optimizing routes. This will be analyzed to see how a mixed solution can improve the global system performance and results by affecting maximum, average, and minimum speeds.

IV. Conclusion and Future Work

In this work we present a model that is evolving to provide a way to represent traffic flow, with different types of vehicles, where we will have the ability to integrate priority vehicles and generate different types of scenario simulations.

Over the last years, there has been significant progress in four key areas: traffic management, route optimization for priority vehicles, agent-based models, and traffic simulation software. However, challenges remain. These include improving efficiency and computing capacity, adapting to the dynamic nature of mobility, and refining model validation and calibration. Calibration and validation techniques vary widely depending on the specific traffic issues and their complexity. Additionally, reproducibility is challenging, as previous models are often difficult to replicate. We must also address the capabilities of open-source solutions for integrating various modules or frameworks to manage transportation systems and control traffic behavior effectively.

The research presented herein has laid a solid foundation for the development of an agent-based model (ABM) focused on urban traffic scenarios, with a particular emphasis on improving mobility for priority vehicles. Through the integration of Geographic Information Systems (GIS) and real-world data, the study has demonstrated the potential of ABM to simulate complex urban traffic dynamics, offering insights into the efficiency of various traffic management strategies under different conditions. The implementation of the model in NetLogo, leveraging GIS data from Open Street Maps, has allowed for the creation of an urban environment that can be adapted for various cities beyond Barcelona. The model's ability to simulate multi-lane traffic systems and incorporate detailed road characteristics has been instrumental in analyzing traffic flow dynamics and will allow assessment of the impact of priority vehicles on overall traffic efficiency.

The preliminary simulation results have provided insights into traffic flow dynamics, highlighting the influence of vehicle acceleration, deceleration, and lane occupancy on traffic fluidity. These findings underscore the importance of considering these factors in urban planning and traffic management strategies, particularly in relation to improving conditions for priority vehicles such as ambulances.

Looking ahead, the next phase of this research will focus on several key areas:

- Enhancing Road Characteristics: Further refinement of the environmental model will involve integrating more detailed road characteristics and traffic signals into the simulation. This will allow for a more accurate representation of real-world conditions and facilitate the analysis of how these elements impact traffic flow and priority vehicle mobility.
- Incorporating Priority Vehicles: The integration of priority vehicles into the model will enable the exploration of various strategies aimed at improving their mobility. This includes the implementation of priority signals, lane reservation, and route optimization techniques. The impact of these strategies on overall traffic flow dynamics will be closely examined.
- Transition to High Performance Computing (HPC): To accommodate larger-scale simulations and more complex scenarios, the model will transition to an HPC environment. This will enhance computational efficiency and allow for the analysis of traffic dynamics across larger urban areas.
- Validation and Calibration: Ongoing efforts will focus on the calibration and validation of the simulation model against real-world data. This will ensure the accuracy of the model's predictions and its applicability to real-world traffic management challenges.

By addressing these areas, the research aims to contribute significantly to the development of effective traffic management strategies that prioritize the mobility of priority vehicles. Ultimately, this work seeks to enhance public safety and operational efficiency across densely populated urban environments, paving the way for smarter and more sustainable cities.

ACKNOWLEDGMENTS

This publication is supported under contract PID2020-112496GB-I00, funded by the Agencia Estatal de Investigacion (AEI), Spain and the Fondo Europeo de Desarrollo Regional (FEDER) UE and partially funded by a research collaboration agreement with the Fundacion Escuelas Universitarias Gimbernat (EUG).

REFERENCES

[1] H. Da˘glayan and M. Karakaya, An Optimized Ambulance Dispatching Solution for Rescuing Injures after Disaster. Univers. J. Eng. Sci., vol. 4, no. 3, pp. 50–57 https://doi.org/10.13189/ujes.2016.040303, 2016

[2] Zhengbo Hao, Yizhe Wang, and Xiaoguang Yang, Every Second Counts: A Comprehensive Review of Route Optimization and Priority Control for Urban Emergency Vehicles, Sustainability, MDPI, vol. 16(7), pages 1-25, March, 2024

[3] González Cuevas, A., and Suppi, R., ABM simulation focused on urban mobility. X Jornadas de Cloud Computing, Big Data & Emerging Topics La Plata, 2022

[4] Pxdraft, Traffic Simulation Systems Market share & Analysis | 2023-2030. Kings Research. https://www.kingsresearch.com/traffic-simulation-systems-market-24, 2023

[5] Gautam Mahajan, Transportation Predictive Analytics and Simulation Market size. https://www.coherentmarketinsights.com/market-insight/transporation-predictive-analytics-and-simulation-market-3180, 2023

[6] Sameer, Mostafa, and Ratrout, Nedal, State of the Art of traffic simulation software. 10.13140/RG.2.2.23572.37764, 2023

[7] Kotusevski, G, and Hawick, Ken, A Review of Traffic Simulation Software. Res. Lett. Inf. Math. Sci., 13, 2009

[8] Weiqi Yu, Weichen Bai, Wenging Luan and Liang Qi, State-of-the-Art Review on Traffic Control Strategies for Emergency Vehicles. IEEE Access, 10, 109729–109742. https://doi.org/10.1109/access.2022.3213798, 2022

[9] Lakshmi, A. V., Sekhar, P. C., Joseph, K. S., and Priya, A, A Systematic Review of route optimization for ambulance routing problem. In Advances in health sciences research (pp. 294–304). https://doi.org/10.2991/978-94-6463-164-7_20, 2023

[10] S. Ahmed, H. A. Hefny, and R. Farid Ibrahim, An Efficient Ambulance Routing System forEmergency Cases based on Dijkstra's Algorithm, AHP, and GIS Exploring Key PerformanceIndicators View project E-government Projects View project An Efficient Ambulance RoutingSystem for Emergency Cases based on Dijkstra's Algorithm, AHP, and GIS https://www.researchgate.net/publication/355062503, 2018

[11] Malleson, N., Birkin, M., Birks, D., Ge, J., Heppenstall, A., Manley, E., McCulloch, J., and Ternes, P., Agent-based modelling for Urban Analytics: State of the art and challenges. AI Communications, 35(4), 393–406. https://doi.org/10.3233/aic-220114, 2022

[12] Heppenstall, A., Crooks, A., Malleson, N., Manley, E., Ge, J., and Batty, M., Future Developments in Geographical Agent-Based Models: Challenges and Opportunities. Geographical Analysis, 53(1), 76–91. https://doi.org/10.1111/gean.12267, 2020

[13] OpenStreetMap Homepage, https://www.openstreetmap.org. Last accessed 29 February, 2024

[14] YOLOv5 Homepage, https://github.com/ultralytics/yolov5. Last accessed 29 February, 2024

[15] NetLogo Homepage, https://ccl.northwestern.edu/netlogo. Last accessed 29 February, 2024

[16] Repast HPC Homepage, https://repast.github.io/repast_hpc.html. Last accessed 29 February, 2024

[17] C. C. Robusto, The cosine-haversine formula, The American Mathematical Monthly, 64(1), 38-40, 1957

[18] S. Mhapankar, A Navigation System for Low-cost Autonomous All-terrain-vehicles, M.Sc. thesis, University of North Carolina at Charlotte, pp. 1-70, 2019.

Predictive AI To Feed Simulation

Carlo Simon, Stefan Haag and Natan Georgievic Badurasvili
Hochschule Worms
Erenburgerstr. 19, 67549 Worms, Germany
e-mail: {simon, haag, natan.badurasvili}@hs-worms.de

***Abstract*—In an industry project, the authors had successfully modelled and simulated the inbound and outbound traffic of a warehouse with the aid of high-level Petri nets. But instead of taking this simulation tool to improve the future planning, the practitioners confronted the authors with another problem: the reasons for the incorrect planning is less the planning process but the inability to foresee which of the scheduled trucks will be late and sabotage the time plan. As a solution to this problem, the authors considered methods of predictive artificial intelligence and especially machine learning. The idea is to take past schedules to train a neural network in order to forecast deviations of upcoming schedules. The paper answers the question on how to extend the previous simulation model by a suitable forecast component which is now ready to be tested with real-world data. The paper explains the scenario of the real-world warehouse, the simulation of its traffic and the information needed for this. Afterwards, the necessary extensions of the data set are explained and how to set up a machine learning component to predict future deviations of schedules. The adapted schedules can then be simulated to create alternative schedules. This is a next step of the authors' research to conduct their simulation on a set of future scenarios in order to chose the schedule that performs not worse than the initial schedule on the original data, but performs better under the alternative scenarios.**

***Keywords*-Predictive Artificial Intelligence; Neural Networks; Machine Learning; Simulation; Petri Nets.**

I. INTRODUCTION

During the SIMUL 2023 conference, the participants had various discussions about the impact of currently discussed Artificial Intelligence (AI) methods like transformers on simulation. While simulation is about causality, many AI methods are about correlation. The participants generally doubted that AI will substitute current simulation methods. However, there is still the possibility to pair both approaches.

For the authors, this discussion happened at the right time, because at this moment they were incapable to solve a problem that arose in an industry project with their currently preferred methods. They could simulate the incoming and outgoing traffic of a large warehouse for registered transports as described in Section II with the aid of a high-level Petri net. But this did not take into account that the registered (planned) arrival time and the actual arrival time of the transports often do not match.

The authors started to identify possible reasons for late transports, such as the transport distance, the shipping agent, the producer or the current weather conditions. All of them did not play a role during the actual simulation of the inbound and outbound traffic of the warehouse.

Unfortunately, the industry partner does not collect information about delays and, hence, cannot provide empirical values. Before asking them to do so, it was the wish of the authors to develop their simulation environment further by adding AI technologies, first. Two possible approaches have been considered initially:

1) Develop an AI that applies compensation strategies comparable to those of the warehouse management if arriving transports are late.
2) Develop an AI that forecasts the expected arrival time of transports on the base of former transportation data.

The first approach has been discarded because this would require a close observation of the current work. The authors did not expect to receive an approval for this.

The second approach, however, seemed to be a natural evolution of work conducted up to now. The idea led to the research question:

How can we extend the previous simulation model by a forecast component based on machine learning?

In this phase of the research, it is not yet the aim to apply the approach to real-world data. It is rather the aim to show the feasibility of the approach, and to develop a framework as a foundation from which concrete industry projects can be processed.

Before explaining the new AI specific components of the simulation environment, the paper continues in Section II with a description of the high-level Petri net simulation model for the inbound and outbound traffic of a warehouse. The authors especially focus on the data needed for simulation. Afterwards, in Section III, a brief introduction is given to the necessary Machine Learning (ML) methods. Both topics are combined in Section IV to define the structure of a possible ML data set for the problem first and to explain the ML approach in Section V next. Section VI demonstrates how to integrate the ML approach into the existing environment. The paper ends in Section VII with a conclusion and an outlook on future work.

II. REAL-WORLD PROBLEM

The industry partner at an industrial park (Industriepark Höchst, *ISL*) provides logistics services for chemical, pharmaceutical and healthcare industries and currently expands its logistics services. Freely published information show the size of this venture [1]:

- Space for more than 21,000 pallets
- 9 separate warehouse sections
- Storage of multiple hazardous material storage classes for chemicals and pharmaceutics
- A wide temperature range from -6 to 20 degrees Celsius in the different sections of the warehouse

As depicted in Figure 1, the warehouse can be accessed via ramps (❷). Each section has a loading zone (❸) and the actual storage zone (❻).

During planning and go live, the inbound and outbound traffic of this warehouse has to be simulated to objectify assumptions made during the conceptual phase. A typical inbound process is conducted as follows: before approaching the industrial park, the shipping agent books a time slot in advance. When trucks arrive, the drivers register with the gatekeeper in the office (❶). Afterwards, they dock at the ramp they have been assigned to (❷). Then, the goods are picked by standard forklifts (called VHS) and placed in the staging zone (❸). After the truck has left, the goods are carried through the driving zone (❹) and dropped on a handover point (❺). Finally, narrow aisle forklifts (called SGS) pick the goods and store them in the high rack storage area (❻).

Outbound processes are executed in reverse order, except that the goods are provided in the staging zone before trucks arrive.

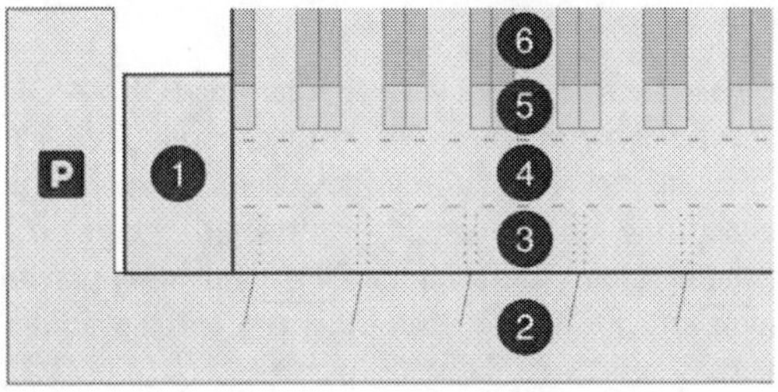

Figure 1. Sketch of the Warehouse.

Various specifics may be excluded from the simulation, such as the commissioning of certain goods. Furthermore, the precise positioning of goods within the warehouse, and consequently the exact driving times, hold diminished importance. In lieu of this, reasonable average times have been selected to replicate typical operational norms.

Model and simulation have been described in detail in [2] and [3]. The model consists of state machines for the inbound and outbound processes and a high-level Petri net to execute these state machines in parallel. Also, time constraints and restricting resources are taken into account.

Two conceptual data models for orders and resources are needed for this. The resources are discussed, first. Table I shows the data needed for simulation based on one kind of resource. This information is spread over several tables (or, in terms of Petri nets, over several places) for each kind of resource.

TABLE I. Attributes for the Resource Places

Attribute	Description
id	id for resources of this kind
product	product group
free	available or locked
timestamp	timestamp of the latest state change
order	assigned order id

Attribute *id* may identify a specific resource like a numbered ramp or a dedicated resource of this kind, like one of the VHS. *product* describes the resource allocation to chemical or pharmaceutical. *order* references to the order that uses this resource and simplifies joins among the different data sets.

Table II shows the data needed for orders. Beside an identifier *id* and the specification whether the order belongs to a chemical or pharmaceutical *product*, the *total* number of pallets for the transport is specified. *status* identifies the current order's state and, implicitly, whether this is an inbound or outbound process.

TABLE II. Attributes of an Order's State

Attribute	Description
id	order id
product	product group
total	total amount of pallets requested
status	initial or current order status
ramp	target ramp
arrival	scheduled time of arrival
preparation	scheduled time of completed staging
fillHandover	amount of pallets in handover areas
fillRamp	amount of pallets at target ramp
fillTruck	amount of pallets in truck
usedGate	used resource *gate*
usedSGS	used resource *SGS*
usedVHS	used resource *VHS*
timestamp	timestamp of the latest state change

One or two times must be defined per order: for both inbound and outbound, the *arrival* time of the truck is given due to its registration. Outbound processes additionally need a *preparation* time when staging begins. This staging time leaves room for optimisation for the warehouse operators.

At the end of the simulation explained in the following, all changes to orders are exported to a dashboard. A *timestamp* traces the moments these changes occur. To simplify the computing of this visualisation, the allocated resources like *ramp*, *usedGate*, *usedSGS*, *usedVHS* are saved. Finally, the amount of goods at the different places is stored in the attributes *fillHandover*, *fillRamp*, and *fillTruck*.

Without having an impact on the result, the real process and the simulated one differ slightly. For the simulation, the ramps are assigned in advance; in real world, the ramp is assigned by the gatekeeper.

The authors have chosen the *Process-Simulations.Center* (*P-S.C*) for modelling and simulation [4]. Since the *P-S.C* is a Petri net based Integrated Management System, it fulfils further constraints important for the industry partner among the pure ability to simulate. Safety and security aspects are of high priority to ISL. Therefore, access to and visibility of (real-world) data must be limited.

The *P-S.C-Cloud* (the *P-S.C* is only provided via internet) and the multi-client capability of the *P-S.C* help to manage security issues [4]: The tool itself only runs locally in a browser with data never leaving the system. Sensitive input data and simulation results can be stored on in-house servers without the *P-S.C-Cloud* ever coming in contact.

In addition, the industry partner requires a user interface (UI) to edit the simulation parameters (orders, times, resources, priorities) easily. The simulation results ought to be presented in a descriptive dashboard. Today, such an interface is called a digital shadow, a piece of software which maps real-world data and processes to a virtual world [5].

Figure 2 explains the interaction between the *P-S.C* and the local UI using CSV-files. Simulation parameters can be imported this way, too.

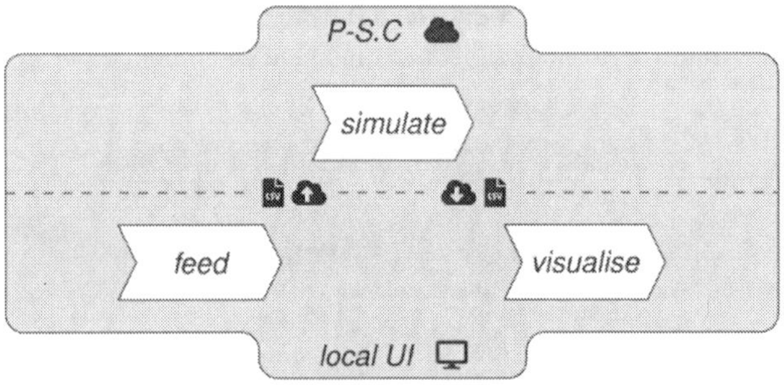

Figure 2. Coupling of Digital Shadow (local UI) and *P-S.C*.

The execution of a specific simulation scenario is divided into three distinct phases:

- **Feed:** The local UI is implemented as a web-based application that can be used with any internet connected computer or iPad. It is used to enter the simulation parameter, priorities and especially the actual order data.
- **Simulate:** The *P-S.C* loads the data into the browser of the end user to start the simulation. The *P-S.C-Cloud* does not get in touch with it which guarantees full control over the data. After the simulation has finished, an automatic download is started and the users can store the results on local hardware.
- **Visualise:** The downloaded file in turn can now be uploaded in a dashboard which is also implemented in the local UI. This helps the end-users to find the best strategy for driving the warehouse. In particular, workload spikes, transportation bottlenecks, and staff occupancy can be analysed and visualised.

This approach is limited to simulate one specific schedule of orders for one specific period, e.g., one day. It is not flexible concerning deviations of the transports. The next sections explain how to extend this environment to handle this limitation.

III. Machine Learning Fundamentals

Artificial Intelligence (AI) is defined in many different ways. These definitions lie in a quadrant chart: one axis denotes the scope of acting and thinking, while the other denotes the spectrum between pure rationality and human semirationality. The most common definition of AI is that of a rational agent. Such an agent tries to provide the best (expected) outcome, given its inputs. What constitutes the best outcome remains a matter of definition [6].

If a rational agent is created to improve the provided output by gaining some sort of experience, this is called Machine Learning (ML). Figure 3 shows the idea of ML as described by [7]. The figure depicts the rational agent as a model. Its task (red) is to compute an output when presented with input data. The model obtains a mapping based on training data. Its formation is the learning problem (blue). Which algorithms are used depends on the choice of ML model [7].

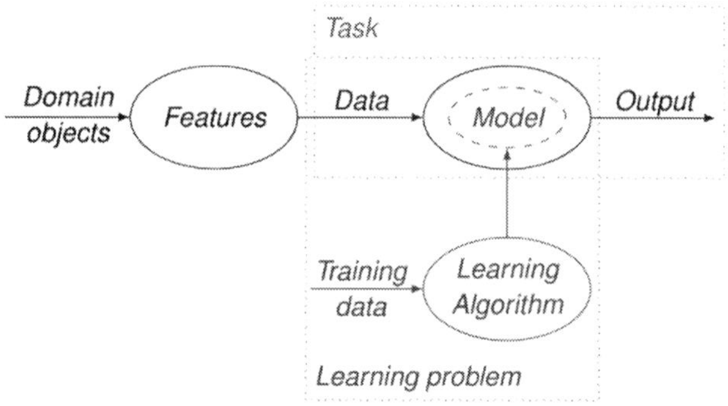

Figure 3. Machine Learning as Explained by [7].

One possible ML model is Deep Learning (DL). A DL model is an artificial neural network with several (hidden) layers. A neural network is to mimic the principle of real neurons. Single neurons are connected by directed, weighted arcs. If the incoming arcs yield a high enough activation potential, the activation function in a neuron triggers a corresponding output. The weighs constitute the main parameters of this ML model type [8].

If the training set includes results, this is called supervised learning. In this case, the data is considered labelled. The metric used to examine the model's quality is to compare the actual results with the computed ones [9].

Two kinds of problems may be solved with the aid of artificial neural networks:

- **Classification:** In mathematical notation, a classifier is a function $y = f(x)$, where x is the input data item and y is the output category [10].
  Applied to our example of a warehouse, classification could help to predict which transports may be unpunctual.
- **Regression:** In regression, we try to understand the data points by discovering the curve that might have generated them [10].
  Applied to our example of a warehouse, regression could help to predict how many minutes transports may be unpunctual.

Both aspects will be discussed in Section V.

IV. Extended Data Set for ML

The aim of the presented approach is to complete future orders and especially to forecast

- which future transports will or will not be in time, i.e., to solve a classification problem, and
- to forecast the expected deviation of the arrival time of future transports, i.e., to solve a regression problem.

But which parameters may influence the arrival time of trucks? And how can this information be coded, such that it can be processed by a learning algorithm?

First, it is worth to consider the data used for simulation already. All "internal" parameters of the orders like order *id*, current *timestamp* of the simulation, allocated *ramp* and other resources (*fillHandover*, *fillRamp*, *fillTruck*, *usedGate*, *usedSGS*, or *usedVHS*), and the *preparation* time for outgoing orders can be ruled out as possible sources.

The probably most valuable source is the planned *arrival* time coded as a timestamp consisting of date and time. This information, which is typically stored as a string, should be preprocessed for a learning algorithm. The following information can be extracted and coded as discrete numbers:

- The month or season of arrival, which may have an impact due to weather conditions.
- The arrival time in hours or at least in categories like early, in the middle of the day or by the end of the day, which may have an impact on the transportation conditions like traffic or the work schedule of the drivers.
- The day of week which may have an impact on the traffic intensity.

Also, the *state* attribute may be of interest because it is used to differ between incoming and outgoing transports. For outgoing transports, "only" an empty truck has to arrive while incoming transports need to be prepared before they reach the warehouse. This might have an impact on the arrival time.

Attribute *product* is not as valuable as supposed by its name. The simulation only distinguishes between chemical and pharmaceutical products which is very rough. It is not obvious that these two categories correlate with a deviation since there are hundreds of different concrete products that belong to these two groups.

Finally, the *total* amount of pallets is a candidate which might have an impact on the arrival time, especially for incoming transports. Large amounts of goods may cause more problems when being loaded compared to smaller ones.

Further attributes might have an impact which are not considered during simulation. The following attributes have been found by the authors:

- The transportation *distance*, especially if a truck has to arrive from outside of the industrial park or whether it is an internal transport.
- The *shipping agents* may differ concerning their quality standards and the accuracy of delivery time.
- Finally, the producer might have an impact on the time a transport can start after being loaded and, hence, whether it arrives on time.

All remaining values can be enumerated and can hence be used for training of a neuronal net.

Unfortunately, the industry partner does not track these additional information. Even the deviation between the planned and the actual arrival time is not documented. Hence, the following considerations are only of theoretical nature.

V. ML FOR PREDICTIVE DEVIATION SCHEDULING

In the context discussed in this paper, Deep Neural Networks (DNNs) can be used threefold. First, they can create yet missing data, thus establishing a means to plan ahead of knowledge. Second, they can predict which transports may be not on time. Third, they can surmise the time deviation.

A. Neural Nets to Complete the Feed

Data becomes worse - or even non-existent - the farther the look into the future. Thus, missing but plausible data has to be integrated into the feed. The corresponding DNN gets trained with historical data of planned arrival times of trucks. From this training data, the net creates fictional yet plausible data entries to complete the fragmentary known data. The thus enriched data constitutes one possible scenario to be analysed by simulation. As it is the first fully scheduled data set, it can be regarded as the base scenario.

B. Neural Nets for Classification

The associated DNN can learn from historical data which deliveries and dispatches were on time. Thus, it can predict the probability of a trip to be delayed or advanced. This is due to the neural nets capability to learn from underlying correlations. Such correlations may be interpreted as questions like:

- Are there shipping agents that often are late?
- Are there producers that always are early?
- Are midweek deliveries more reliable than ones on Mondays?

After establishing the probabilities of unpunctuality, alternative scenarios can be established. These scenarios incorporate differing yet still plausible delay and advance times. The corresponding schedules can then be compared to the base scenario.

C. Neural Nets for Regression

Knowing which delivery may be late is one side of the coin. The other is the actual time. The fitting DNN can make guesses about these times. Again, the capabilities of neural nets to represent correlations prove useful: Several different effects may overlap that may add up to massive delays. An example for this may be an unreliable hauler in the midst of winter on an early Monday morning. These time delta represent the last puzzle piece in creating alternative scenarios.

D. Implementation Insights

As a tool only provided via internet, the architecture of the *P-S.C-Cloud* consists of a JavaScript client and a PHP Server. The prototypical implementation of a ML component to conduct the previously described tasks is done with Python instead. The reason for this is the existence of a large number of ML libraries that can simply be combined. Especially the following packages are used [11]:

- **NumPy** provides data types and functions for easier handling of complex structures, such as vectors and matrices.

- **pandas** is designed for more complex structures and their easy handling. One strength is its extensive functionality for table structures.
- **Matplotlib** is used for visual analyses and plotting.
- **scikit-learn** contains many ML algorithms that can be easily used in your own program.
- **Keras** can build artificial neural networks.
- **TensorFlow** extends Keras with additional well performing functionalities and can handle large and complex data structures.

With the goal to train a DNN as an example, typical delivery information including possible delays, have been guessed in a students' project. While some of the information have been randomised, others include pattern like specific shipping agents always being late.

The numerical representation of the input data is partially generated in the JavaScript part of the implementation, others make use of the predefined ML algorithms in Python.

The derived information concerning completed order lists, classification and regression are currently produced in the Python environment. They can be stored in CSV files which can then be integrated into the *P-S.C-Cloud* via file upload.

VI. ML Extended Simulation

It is the aim to integrate the ML solution presented in the previous section into the formerly introduced simulation environment as shown in Figure 4. After the trusted orders are entered for simulation, a new phase **refurbish** is executed which makes use of the ML model.

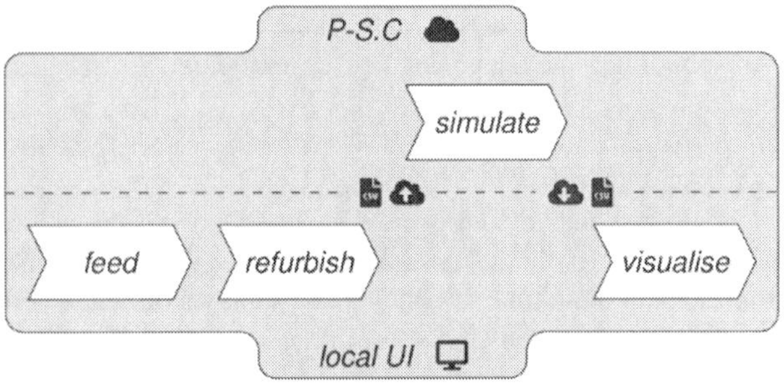

Figure 4. Simulation environment extended by ML.

With the goal to improve the ramp allocation, simulation is conducted in two phases. Figure 5 shows the improved planning approach.

A. Simulation of a Planned Schedule

In the first iteration, the orders are simulated for the case that all transports arrive as planned. If further orders are expected for the simulation period, the ML algorithm is able to generate plausible orders with respect to the known order history.

The simulation is conducted with the goal to find an optimal ramp allocation which reduces idle times for the shipping companies combined with a minimal labour utilisation. Different ramp allocations may lead to almost same results.

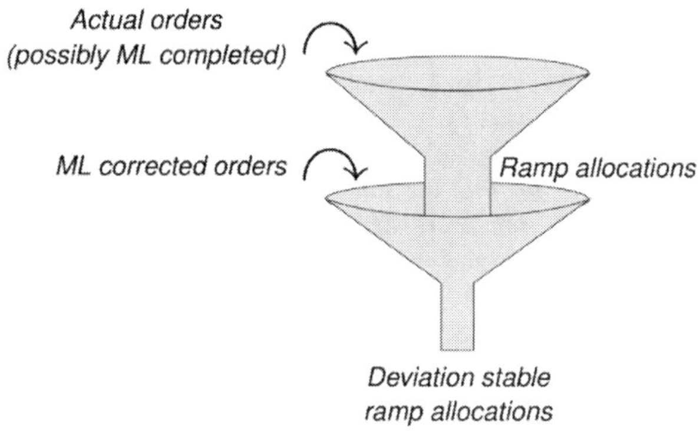

Figure 5. Two-Phase approach for ramp allocation.

B. Simulation of a Planned Schedule plus (DNN) Delays

During the second phase, the orders are corrected with respect to the assumed deviations of transport times. The ramp allocation strategies found in the first phase are applied to these adapted schedules and evaluated with respect to the optimisation criteria. These simulation results are used as a filter to find that allocation strategy which fits best to the original and the adapted orders.

C. Preliminary Work of Industry Partners

As mentioned before, the industry partner does not collect information needed for the machine learning approach. To prepare data collection, the training data mentioned before is divided into three classes:

- **Available:** timestamp of the planned arrival; incoming vs. outgoing transports; amount of pallets
- **Not available but collectable:** the delay of transports; transportation distance in the sense of transports inside the industry park or nor; the shipping agent; the producer
- **Not available and not collectable:** in advance, the transportation distance in length

This classification reinforces the appraisal that the introduced approach can be conducted. It's application depends on the willingness of the industry partners.

VII. Conclusion and Outlook

As initially stated, the goal of this research is to provide an environment to improve simulation in logistics. It uses machine learning based techniques to create schedules that are (mostly) indifferent to deviations from the original planning. Thus, a good schedule performs at least as good on the original data as the original schedule; but it performs as good as possible under differing scenarios.

A prototypical environment has been implemented, but the parts are not fully integrated yet. The reason for this is that the industry partner does not collect information of the deviation of planned and actual arriving time of the trucks. Also, other information that could help to train a neural net are not considered by the partner. The possibility to do so, has been explained above.

This is the next important research step for the authors: check the approach with real-world data! Afterwards it makes sense to develop the integration further.

Even with this approach it is not possible to know which transports will be late in the future. But the developed scenario is more stable with respect to delays in delivery without degrading the initial plan. And for checking this plan, simulation is still needed. Statistical estimations are insufficient for processes in logistics.

REFERENCES

[1] Infraserv Logistics GmbH, *Overview hazardous substances warehouse*, https://www.infraserv-logistics.com/en/isl/news/news/ (last accessed 08.2024), 2023.

[2] L. Zakfeld, C. Simon, S. Hladik, and S. Haag, "Real World Case Study To Teach Simulation", in *SIMUL 2023: The Fifteenth International Conference on Advances in System Simulation*, Valencia (Spain), 2023, pp. 19–24.

[3] C. Simon and S. Haag, "Pairing Finite Automata and Petri nets - Simulation of Processes in Logistics", in *ECMS 2024: 38th International ECMS Conference on Modelling and Simulation*, D. Grzonka, N. Rylko, and G. S. V. Mityushev, Eds., Krakow (Poland), 2024, pp. 474–480.

[4] C. Simon, S. Haag, and L. Zakfeld, "The Process-Simulation.Center", in *SIM-SC: Special Track at SIMUL 2022: The Fourteenth International Conference on Advances in System Simulation*, F. Herrmann, Ed., Lisbon (Portugal), 2022, pp. 74–77.

[5] T. Bergs *et al.*, "The Concept of Digital Twin and Digital Shadow in Manufacturing", *Procedia CIRP*, vol. 101, pp. 81–84, 2021, 9th CIRP Conference on High Performance Cutting, ISSN: 2212-8271.

[6] S. Russell and P. Norvig, *Artificial Intelligence - A Mordern Approach*, 4th ed. London: Pearson, 2021.

[7] P. Flach, *Machine Learning - The Art and Science of Algorithms that Make Sense of Data*, 9th ed. Cambridge: Cambridge University Press, 2012.

[8] J. Howard and S. Gugger, *Deep Learning for Coders with fastai & PyTorch*. Sebastopol: O'Reilly, 2020.

[9] A. Géron, *Hands-on Machine Learning with Scikit-Learn, Keras & TensorFlow*. Sebastopol: O'Reilly UK Ltd., 2019.

[10] C. Mattmann, Ed., *Machine Learning with TensorFlow*, 2nd ed. Shelter Island, NY: Manning, 2020.

[11] M. Karatas, *Development of AI applications (in German: Eigene KI-Anwendungen programmieren)*. Bonn: Rheinwerk Computing, 2024.